The Wallowas

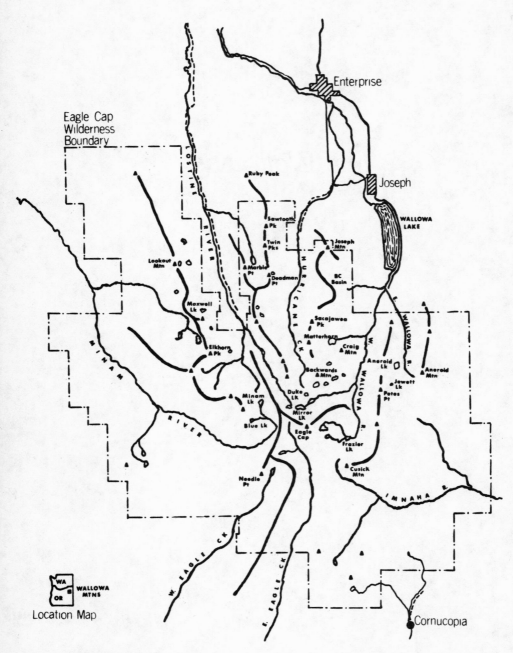

Eagle Cap
Wilderness
Boundary

Enterprise

Joseph

WALLOWA
LAKE

▲ Ruby Peak

Sawtooth
▲ Pk

Twin
▲ Pks

▲ Joseph
Mtn

BC
Basin

Marble
▲ Pt

▲ Deadman
Pt

Lookout
Mtn

Maxwell
Lk

Sacajawea
▲ Pk

Matterhorn

Elkhorn
▲ Pk

▲ Craig
Mtn

Aneroid
Lk

▲ Aneroid
Mtn

Backwards
▲ Mtn

Jewett
Lk

Minam
Lk

▲ Pates
Pt

Duke
Lk

Blue Lk

Mirror
Lk

Eagle
Cap

▲ Frazier
LK

Cusick
▲ Mtn

Needle
▲ Pt

Cornucopia

WA
OR
WALLOWA
MTNS

Location Map

Map prepared by William B. Purdom
Department of Geology.
Southern Oregon State College

The Wallowas

Coming of Age
in the Wilderness

by William Ashworth

HAWTHORN BOOKS, INC.

A Howard & Wyndham Company

NEW YORK

ALSO BY WILLIAM ASHWORTH:

HELLS CANYON: THE DEEPEST GORGE ON EARTH

Library of Congress Catalog Card Number: 77-70121
ISBN: 0-8015-8371-3
1 2 3 4 5 6 7 8 9 10

For Stan,
who'll get there yet

Westward the Oregon flows and the Walloway and Owyhee. . . .
　　　　　　　—Henry Wadsworth Longfellow, *Evangeline*

Prologue

There are three major stages of awareness that may be passed through as an individual develops a relationship with wild country.

The first stage may be called *adventure*. In this stage, wilderness is looked upon as an adversary, to be met, battled, and defeated (by boot, by bulldozer; the difference in means is not materially significant). Most people, I am convinced, never pass beyond this rudimentary and incomplete beginning.

The second stage may be called *understanding*. Here the wilderness is not an adversary but something more akin to a schoolroom, in which questions are asked and reasons are sought. What made this valley the shape it is? Why is there a lake here? What kind of flower is that, and why is it growing up here in these rocks? Why is there a timberline?

The third stage is, in many ways, merely a continuation of the second, and nearly all of those who pass beyond adventure will eventually enter into it. It is the stage in which answers begin to be known. Now the wilderness is seen not as an adversary or a schoolroom but as patterns—patterns that have value not for what they can provide to humanity but simply for themselves. And though in order to see these patterns an individual must relinquish his powerful position as lord and master of the world, when he has done so he will feel larger—not smaller—than before. He no longer stands on top of the universe, he embraces it. He is not *in* the world, but *of* it, integrated and complete and whole.

This final stage may be called *peace*.

Adventure

I

On Cliff Olin's nineteenth birthday—less than one week after *my* nineteenth birthday—the two of us spent all of the latter half of the afternoon climbing a mountain backwards. Or maybe you could say we climbed it upside down. Anyway, we began at the top, scrambled most of the way to the bottom, and then turned around and climbed to within ten feet of the top again.

Perhaps I had better back up a bit and explain. We were in the Wallowas. We had been in the Wallowas for three days. It was early, flawless August. There was a canteen with a missing lid. . . .

That particular mountain hadn't been on the agenda at all, in the beginning. This was to be a rambling day, a roaming day, a let's-what's-over-the-next-rise-and-to-hell-with-the-trail day; nobody had put any climbing into it that I knew of. The mountains were to be our backdrop, not our stage. That was the plan. But the plan did not account for the fact that Cliff and I were barely nineteen.

The day had begun early, as most days do in the mountains. It had begun with no sun in the sky, only a patch of light and a promise beyond the eastern rim of the basin which would soon become the sun. The light was gray in camp, and the gray light was cold. We got up rapidly; we built a fire, with the urgency and clumsiness of cold hands. Below us, wrapping us on three sides, Mirror Lake lapped blackly at polished granite.

Cliff and I were half of a party of four—all in our late teens, unchaperoned, buoyed by the mountain air and boisterous with the success of our assault on Eagle Cap the previous day. We were camped at what is very nearly the westernmost lake in the Lake Basin, on the south shore, only there wasn't a south shore; only talus and great dark cliffs and, halfway along, a rocky, sheer-sided little peninsula with a spring at its base and a single gnarled tree at its tip and barely enough room for four sleeping bags on its level, matted summit. The day stretched before us; the day beckoned. What lakes would we see, what cliffs and what green meadows?

The sun crept down the mountains. The sun raced down the mountains, but we were faster. The sun found an empty camp and, a hundred yards to the east, four tiny figures leaping from boulder to giant boulder along the southern margin of the water.

We passed a tall waterfall, negotiated a bog, rounded the southeast corner of the lake, and came out on the east shore. Here was a marvel—a great, broad slab of polished granite, hundreds of square feet in extent, smooth as a table but tilted sharply and plunging into the lake to continue unchanged to what depths we could not tell. Beyond the slab was scattered open timber; and beyond the timber was the outlet stream, tumbling and whirling through meadows on its way to the next lake in the chain, Moccasin, a half mile distant and some two hundred feet below. There is a trail between Mirror and Moccasin lakes, but it doesn't follow the stream. We did. The way was alternately easy, alternately nearly impossible. At one point we came out at the top of a thirty-foot cliff; a hundred feet to the left, fifty feet to the right, it could easily be bypassed. Two members of the party did just that. The other two—Cliff and I—were not to be that easily turned aside. We found a chimney and scrambled directly down.

What good are the mountains if you don't find adventure in them?

We were at Moccasin by midmorning. I have heard it said since that Moccasin Lake is the most beautiful spot in the Wallowa Mountains. I am sorry to say that I can neither confirm nor deny that statement; here in this mountain morning of sun and little winds, my imagination was fixed not upon beauty but upon a rock. A marvelous great rock, a huge rock. Fifty feet long if it was an inch, and dead level, it thrust toward the heart of the lake like some gigantic monolithic causeway, its top pavement smooth, its sides sheer, and with water lapping all round it a constant three inches down from its square, quarried-looking edge. At its lakeward end, clear water darkened to blue-black unimaginable depths. It would have been a perfect diving platform, but the air was not yet warm and the water was frigid. We talked about it, but no one made the first move.

Now our way led north, again without benefit of trail, up a steep green hillside among trees and scattered small outcrops of brilliant, gray-white granite. At the top, a surprise: a tiny lake, hardly more than a pond, cupped on three sides by meadow and timber and on the fourth—the west—by a small cliff and an immature talus slope. The water was warmer than the water of Moccasin Lake; having climbed two hundred and fifty feet in the direct heat of the sun, we were warmer too. Three of us stripped and plunged. The fourth—Cliff —disappeared into the woods for a moment, came back in maroon swimming trunks, and was properly hooted. We quickly found that *warmer* was a comparative and not an absolute term. Years later, at a little lake far back in the trackless Siskiyous, a friend and I would decide not to swim because we might, as he put it, "freeze our peepees off." The description is apt. There in the August noon, with the sun beating down and the temperature reaching 100 degrees on the plains around the Wallowas, the four of us froze our peepees off. Afterwards, a bask on sunbaked blocks of talus, the Matterhorn towering in white splendor to one hand, Eagle Cap rais- ing its half-dome-shaped head to the other, nameless mountains— nameless to us, anyway—crowding the rest of the horizon. We had lunch and washed it down with lemonade made from the lake water in Bob Lawrence's green plastic canteen. At that time the canteen still had a lid.

Up to and through lunch, our little lake had been nameless; but now, just as we were leaving, we found a sign nailed to a tree. The sign said "Duke Lake." In some subtle way, this bothered me. Until that moment, we had been explorers, seeking a way through trackless terrain, conquering it with our boots. We had been emperors; we had been pioneers. Now, with the discovery of a small rectangle of wood six inches by nine inches with eight runes marked upon it, we were suddenly demoted. We had discovered somebody else's Duke Lake; we had eaten lunch by somebody else's Duke Lake; we had swum in and had frozen our peepees off in somebody else's Duke Lake. I don't think the sun dimmed in the sky, but I know that a certain nagging aura of disappointment crept upon me, and I suspect that this aura was at least indirectly responsible for what followed.

What followed didn't follow immediately, though. We merely walked northward, through open conifer forest, until we came without suddenness to the north rim of our small plateau and looked down upon Douglas Lake.

Douglas Lake is a large, irregular sheet of blue surrounded by green trees. On three sides, the trees give way to other trees. But on the fourth side—the north side—things are different, were different. I stared. Here the trees humped themselves into a slope, and the slope leaped into a cliff, and the cliff—O heart!—thrust itself, shot itself, two thousand precipitous feet upward from the lake, crowned by a sequence of jagged, wicked-looking pinnacles. Quick, I breathed, the name? A map was consulted. The peak had no name, nothing but an elevation—8,945. No name? Then unexplored, unconquered! And I could be an explorer again.

"I," I announced firmly, "am going to climb that mountain. This afternoon."

"You," announced Cliff, just as firmly, "are a bloody damned fool."

We held a rapid conference. Cliff, despite his deprecating statement, was anxious to accompany me. Bob would come along if Ron Wolff would. Ron Wolff wouldn't. So the party would be split two ways: Ron and Bob to go back to camp, Cliff and I to climb The Mountain. Bob promised to have supper ready when we got back. He handed me his green plastic canteen; I stuck it on my belt. I think we shook hands all around. Cliff and I moved off downslope toward Douglas Lake.

It was three o'clock in the afternoon.

I filled the canteen at a small waterfall tumbling out of the woods at the west end of Douglas Lake, and with that wet weight sloshing against my right hip, hurried to catch Cliff, who was already striding across the narrow neck of land separating Douglas from nearby

Crescent Lake. Our plan of attack was simple. That awesome Douglas Lake wall is split, in several places, by *couloirs,* shallow, steep gullies, reaching from ridge crest to base. We intended to scramble up one of the couloirs on the western end of the face, attain the easy-looking west ridge, and run the ridge to the summit. If all went well, we would be on top by five o'clock and back in camp sometime between seven-thirty and eight.

Crossing the isthmus between the two lakes, we moved up the easy slope to the base of the nearest couloir. The mountain began with startling immediacy. One moment it was brushy slope; the next, hard gray stone, sheer and towering. But the couloir would be a route. It ended some six to ten feet above the base of the cliff, but the rock was good and offered no more than a moderate challenge; soon we were in the gully itself, scrambling upward. I suppose that narrow band of rock at the bottom should have warned me about what was coming later, but if it was a warning I paid no attention to it. We climbed toward the ridge.

The couloir was steep, but its floor was of soft, sandy earth that made climbing ridiculously easy. A good kick would provide a nonslip foothold. We made rapid progress. The couloir opened out near the top, like a funnel; the grade decreased; and soon we were stepping out on the ridge. On the far side, a magnificent view opened out over the Hurricane Canyon and beyond it to the Matterhorn. We stood in a small sandy meadow, level and almost perfectly circular, perhaps fifteen feet in diameter. What a spot for a camp! I immediately espoused the notion of going back, getting Bob and Ron, and dragging them up here, forcibly if necessary, to spend the night. Cliff rudely pricked my bubble. An overnight camp needs water; where, among all these sand particles and god-forsaken rocks, would we find water? We sat on a stone and shared half the canteen. The sun was westering. It was time to push on.

The ridge had weathered into great, tumbled, teetery boulders, ranging from the size of an automobile to the size of a small house. In the spaces between the boulders grew trees, only at this elevation they weren't trees at all but *krummholz,* stiff, matted brush, bearing needles like trees but barely knee-high. Over and around the boulders, around and through the brushlike trees, we climbed, sweating. The sea of mountains grew around us; the lakes and meadows of the Lake Basin receded and fell away. Cliff, with more experience in these matters, began to pull in front of me. His red shirt bobbed and danced among the boulders. It disappeared. The summit—where in hell was the summit? I clambered over boulders. I was profoundly tired of boulders. The ridge curved up, down, up again. A pinnacle beckoned; the wrong one. Another pinnacle, higher this time, with a red-shirted figure sitting on it and dangling its legs over a thousand feet of nothing. "Cliff," I hollered hoarsely, "is that it?"

"Sure is," he answered placidly. "Come on up."

The first thing I noticed, on reaching Cliff's side, was the cairn —someone had built a cairn on my untrammeled summit. The second thing was the view. Like the cairn, it was vaguely disappointing. There was the Lake Basin, of course, spread out beneath us like the proverbial map. But we had seen it spreading as we climbed, and we had seen the same thing from Eagle Cap the previous day; and unlike Eagle Cap, this mountain was not high enough to allow us to see over the basin's ring of encircling mountains. On the way up we had seen Hurricane Canyon and the Matterhorn, but now they were gone, hidden behind an intervening ridge. To the east, no cliffs, only a ridge like the one we had climbed, and on its north side, five hundred feet of fine, sandlike scree dropping into a basin. On the far side of the basin was a small, undistinguished lake.

Only directly at our feet was the view worthy of the effort we had put into it. Here cliffs and crags fell away, dark and brooding and seemingly bottomless. Here a steep, gloomy couloir rent the face, snaking to a small saddle within ten feet of our pinnacle. This was Wild and Real and The Way Mountains Should Be.

We sat on a ledge on the east side of the summit, out of the wind, and shared the last of our water. The Great Couloir yawned beneath us. It was a quarter till six, or a quarter after six—I don't remember which.

"Cliff," I said suddenly, "Let's not go back the way we came. Let's go down the face."

He stared at me. I pointed. "This couloir," I said, "doesn't look much rougher than the one we came up. It ought to take us right to the bottom, a lot quicker than going back down those boulders.

Besides, then we can tell people we climbed the face of this thing. We don't have to tell them we were climbing *down.*"

Cliff nodded. "OK," he said slowly. "Only you go first."

"Me?"

"Then when you start slipping I can go back the other way."

Actually, though, it was Cliff who entered the couloir first. He led the way cautiously down the steep, scree-covered slope from the saddle. The couloir beckoned. We couldn't see the bottom, but everything was saw looked easily passable. We eased downward in deepening shadows, the white scree gray under our feet. Two or three times we reached small bands of steep, slick rock, four to five feet high; each took long moments to negotiate. The cliffs stood over us, raised over us, towered over us. The evening air blew up from the valley, fresh-scented and cold.

We were making excellent time; soon we would be down. The bottom approached. The bottom was there, only it wasn't the bottom. *Now* what? The damn gully had given out, left us stranded forty feet above the base of the cliff. It might as well have been forty miles—we couldn't cross it. To either side were more cliffs. Behind us was the thousand-foot scree slope we had just descended. It was seven o'clock in the evening. "Now," I repeated, "what?"

"If we had a rope—" said Cliff. But we didn't.

I took the cliffs to the west, Cliff the ones to the east. We moved out of the safety of the couloir onto the open rock, looking for alternate routes down. None appeared. It began to look as though the only way out of the situation was back up and over. But neither of us wanted to do that. Dislodged pebbles rattled away down the face. That was one way to descend, of course, but somehow I wasn't *that* anxious to avoid a climb. I turned back. We would simply have to grit our teeth and go back up the stupid mountain and down the way we had come. And hope we made it before dark. And may the fleas of ten thousand camels nest in your beard, you goddamn hunk of rock.

It was at about this point that I dropped the canteen.

We were back in the center of the couloir, taking a last look over the brink before turning away from it to trudge the thousand feet back up the mountain. I don't know exactly how it happened— perhaps my elbow brushed against the canteen, or possibly it struck a rock as I turned. At any rate, one moment the hollow, round bulk of the thing was against my thigh and the next moment it was rolling away down the mountain. It slid through the scree, teetered on the brink, and plunged.

And stopped. No sound of falling. The mountain was silent.

I peered cautiously over the lip of the cliff. There lay the canteen, lodged on a ledge seven or eight feet down, tantalizingly close. Even so, had it been mine, I probably would have left it there. But it was not mine; it was Bob's. Didn't I have a responsibility to get it back to him?

"I'm going to try to climb down there," I said. "Wait for me."

Cliff had already started up the couloir. He whirled around. "What! *You* can't—"

Perhaps it was the way he accented the word *you*. Up to that point, I had been unsure myself that the thing could be done. But now determination arose in me. My unexplored lake had a sign by it, my untrammeled summit had a cairn on it, my way down the mountain had a cliff at the bottom of it, and by god I *would* get that canteen! "Wait," I repeated. "I'll only be a moment." And I moved out onto the cliff.

The climb down proved easier than I had feared. Face to the cliff, I eased downward on good holds. Out fifteen feet to the left; back toward the center, on a four-inch-wide ledge that sloped reassuringly inward. Soon I was sliding cautiously down beside the canteen, picking it up, slipping the clip firmly over my belt.

So far, so good. Now to get back.

There had been no way to climb straight down to the ledge where the canteen lay, but perhaps I could climb straight up. My head was level with the rounded lip. I brought both arms up—carefully, lest the motion throw me off balance and off the mountain—and reached for holds. I found them. But I couldn't use them—the blasted canteen was in my way, getting between me and the mountain. Obviously, the thing to do was to toss it up into the couloir, where Cliff could retrieve it. Let *him* carry it for a while. I removed it from my belt and lobbed it lightly upward. It struck a rock and bounced back. Instinctively, I dodged—and watched it fly past my shoulder, outward, and down. This time there was no ledge to break the fall. It made a beautiful parabolic arc (I had just taken freshman physics, I knew about parabolic arcs), whistled good-bye, and disappeared.

Now, once more, what?

I scrambled up beside Cliff. "We *have* to get that canteen," I found myself saying. "Come on." And without further ado I began racing up the couloir. Cliff followed, no doubt wondering if I had lost my mind, which in a sense I had. We skittered up the scree. A thousand feet an hour is supposed to be good climbing time; we made *this* thousand feet in a little over fifteen minutes. At the saddle, I hesitated only long enough to make sure Cliff was following, then plunged down the northeast scree slope. My plan, which I had explained over my shoulder to Cliff on the way up, was to circle around the eastern flank of the mountain and come back along the base of the cliffs, looking for the spot where the canteen had landed. Just before leaving the bottom of the couloir, I had fixed certain landmarks in my mind—a rock outcrop, a distinctive tree, the shape of Douglas Lake from that angle. The main thing that worried me was approaching night. Would we get around the mountain while there was still light to see those things? The small lake to the northeast, which we had spotted earlier from the summit, had become a black blob on a gray background, only the crags above it still distinct. The crags were golden, and the gold was fading. Half running, half sliding in the loose scree, we raced downward.

I remember very little about the eastern side of the peak or about the terrain along the bottom of the south face. There were large boulders, like the ones we had climbed over on the west ridge. The trees were tree size again. Toward the center of the south face there was a flange of clean, nearly level rock between the boulders and the cliffs, and we stuck mostly to that. The half-light, incredibly, was still hanging on.

After awhile I became convinced that we had passed the spot where the canteen had to be and insisted on going back, and climbing up, if necessary, to look for it again. Cliff had had enough. "All right," he said. "*You* go back and look. *I'll* wait here." And he stretched out flat on his back on a convenient boulder and put his hands behind his head.

I backtracked seventy-five to one hundred yards and began

scrambling up. There were no boulders here, only bare rock, steepening gradually as it changed from slope to face. Soon I was using my hands as well as my feet. I paused every few moments to look around. There was no canteen, only rock and more rock, and—far below me now—Cliff lying on his boulder, his red shirt a blurred and fading accent in the almost-dark.

And then, suddenly, a little further up the face, there *was* the canteen.

I climbed three more steps, reached up, and plucked the thing from its perch. "*You* have caused enough trouble for a while," I told it. "Now stay here." And I shoved the clip over my belt.

The lid was missing, lost in the fall and bounced away God knows where. I didn't look for it; it was enough to have recovered the canteen. Far below me, almost invisible in the deepening gloom, Cliff waited on his boulder. It would take us more than an hour to reach camp. We had better get moving.

Casting a last glimpse backward at the cliff we hadn't climbed, I started down.

I presume the first stars came out as we threaded our way through the timber on the lower flank of the mountain and skirted the west shore of Douglas Lake, but I was too tired to notice. I know it was almost totally dark by the time we reached the trail. Horses were vague shapes in a nearby meadow. A sign—there was barely enough light to make it out—read "Mirror Lake 3."

I remember very little of the trip home to camp. I do recall thinking how odd it was to be able to refer to a place as home when I had been there only two nights. It was too dark to pick out details along the trail. Occasionally, shapes would loom up in the blackness—the ghost of a rock outcrop, the ghost of a tree trunk. There may have been a moon, but I didn't have the energy to look for it. Home was a stony little peninsula jutting out into black water and a great protecting cliff and a fire burning and one lone tree. I thought of the dinner Bob had promised to have ready, and I felt the reassuring weight of his canteen that I had recovered bobbing against my hip, and I put one foot in front of the other.

And again.

And again.

And again.

II

The trip had begun long before its beginning.

I grew up in the university town of Pullman, Washington, in the heart of the Palouse country, one of the richest wheat-producing areas in the world. Hill after golden hill, valley after golden valley, the wheat rolled away to the horizon; the town was awash with it. I wanted mountains. Safe in my room, the wheat locked out, I would read of mountains: *The Journals of Lewis and Clark*; a book called *National Parks in Portfolio*; another called *Little Masterpieces of Science,* which contained, cradled among dry technical tomes, a magnificent adventure story—"The Ascent of Mount Tyndall." In an ancient thirty-volume *Book of Knowledge* I found a long and detailed account of a climb up Mont Blanc. I pored over maps, I devoured Richard Halliburton, and I drowned in wheat.

The Wallowas offered an escape. Invisible and tantalizing, they hung below the southern horizon; first as a pair of tiny triangles in the upper right-hand corner of a gas station map of Oregon, marked "Sacajawea 10,033" and "Matterhorn 10,002"; then as the name "Wallowa Mtns" spread in a ragged arc across that section of the official Oregon State highway map, but with no peak names and no elevations; and finally as a Great Unknown, a blank spot in my knowledge that seemed impossible to fill in. Tantalizing hints were all I had. Here was a picture on the front of a road map, labeled "Wallowa Mountains"; there, an advertising spot on a Lewiston, Idaho, radio station inviting me to visit "Wallowa Lake

Lodge—in the Switzerland of America." But nowhere a complete account, nowhere a picture that offered more than a glimpse. I climbed to the top of Kamiak Butte, a rocky little knob near Pullman, and turned my eyes south. Miles beyond the horizon, the mountains beckoned.

By the time I was halfway through high school, I was hooked. The Wallowas had become an obsession.

Picture, if you will, an area roughly the size and shape of the city of Los Angeles. Within the boundaries of that area, place 126 peaks, each over eight thousand feet high, with at least a dozen approaching ten thousand feet. Separate the peaks by canyons, eleven of them, three to six thousand feet deep and bearing the characteristic U-shaped cross section that is the mark of extensive glacial action. Scar the sides and the summits of the peaks with innumerable cirques, large and small, banked with snow and cupping a total of nearly one hundred fifty lakes. Sprinkle with meadows, and sprinkle the meadows with springs and leaping creeks. Now take a gigantic ice-cream scoop, more than a mile wide, and gouge a three-mile-long chunk out of the center of this jumbled mass of peaks, lakes, springs, creeks, meadows, and canyons. Floor the basin that results with white granite, and decorate it with lakes and trees. Set the whole thing down in a remote corner of Oregon, right beside the deepest canyon on the North American continent, and wrap it in wave after wave of impenetrable, timbered canyons. . . .

I will lift up mine eyes into the hills.

A U.S. Forest Service map offered the following: "The intrusion of the granite Wallowa Batholith probably occurred during the Cretaceous period (125 to 190 million years ago). The molten rock of the batholith forced its way up though the greenstones, pushed the sedimentary rocks aside, and folded them intensely, causing the present contorted limestone formations. The next great chapter in the geological history of the Wallowa region. . . ."

Remember thy Creator in the days of thy youth.

I finished high school and went away to college—Whitman College, in nearby Walla Walla. I took physics, mathematics, English, German, art. The year passed slowly; I dreamed of Great Adventures. Weeks were spent planning a summer-long bicycle trip to Grand Canyon. It perished for lack of funds. A climb of Mt. Rainier? I had long dreamed of mountain climbing, but my only experience to date had been a few piddling little quartzite outcrops on Kamiak. A canoe trip through the San Juan Islands? A visit to the Forbidden Plateau in British Columbia? *National Parks in Portfolio* had come away with me to college, and as spring advanced I began to turn to it far more often than to my textbooks. I got average to below-average grades; I lay on the bank of College Creek, reading and writing poetry, absorbing warm sun and grass scent and the lilting odor of exuberant, heavy lilacs. The Wallowas? The Wallowas?

Summer came. I went home and got a job washing test tubes in a laboratory at Washington State University.

At Whitman I had met Cliff Olin, classmate in physics, table-mate in the dormitory dining room, and companion on many bicycle jaunts about the back roads near Walla Walla. Six days younger than I and about three inches short of my six-foot height, Cliff had a round, close-cropped blond head and a stocky, almost soft-looking body. He was, however, anything but soft. His home was in Port Townsend, Washington, a small old town just at the inner end of the Straits of Juan de Fuca, with its feet in salt water but with the Olympic Mountains poised like a cloud behind it. From his earliest youth, Cliff's eyes had turned toward that cloud; by the time I met him, much of the cloud had resolved itself to rock beneath his questing feet. He was as enamored of mountains and climbing and Great Adventures as I. We became close friends.

That was at Whitman. Now it was summer. Day followed day, test tube followed test tube, each much like the one preceding. I wrote to Cliff: What about a climbing trip in the Wallowas this August? He wrote back: An excellent plan! When do we start?

I was committed. Now I would have to follow through. Nineteen years of dreams were about to coalesce into a reality.

III

It is important to understand the naïveté with which I approached this first venture into the Wallowas and the romantic nature of the concepts that were playing about in my head at the time.

Though I had long been enamored of mountain climbing, I had only the foggiest knowledge of what mountain climbers actually did. I did not know what an ice axe looked like, or a pair of crampons; had never heard of a carabiner; had never handled—much less worn—a backpack. I had some vague notion that mountain climbers tied themselves together with a rope; why I had no idea. Mountain climbers also wore lederhosen and wool sweaters, clung to impossible places on cliffs, and yodeled a lot. They did exciting things and went places where nobody else could get to and got oohed and ahhed over by everyone. I could hardly wait to become one.

Backpackers, now—backpackers were another matter. I had a hard time understanding backpackers. Backpackers were strange, masochistic sorts who went into areas where there were no roads, simply—it seemed—for the pleasure of going into them. They carried lots of things on their backs and got blisters; they looked at the mountains, but did not climb them, either because they were afraid to or because (and this I simply could not begin to fathom) they didn't want to. I was not so sure I wanted to be a backpacker. I could *see* mountains quite adequately, I thought, from a road. In fact, it was my studied opinion that they should build roads right to the bases of all mountains, so that mountain climbers could start directly from their cars. I was not afraid of backpacking, I simply could see no reason for it. Why walk any farther than you absolutely had to?

Despite these superior and rather puzzled opinions concerning backpacking, however, it was to a backpacker that I now turned for assistance—an old friend named Bob Lawrence, who had been a year behind me through high school. A slightly built seventeen-year-old with a Teddy Roosevelt smile and an almost incredible amount of stamina, Bob was easily the most experienced out-doorsman I knew, and the only one of my acquaintance who had actually *been* to the Wallowas. He had been packing into them with his father and brothers for several years. Would he go in now with Cliff and me, show us to a mountain, act as our climbing guide once we got onto it?

He would. I turned the bulk of the planning over to him and returned to the Wallowas of my dreams.

The details of the trip now took shape rapidly under Bob's expert hand. The date was set for the first weekend in August, Friday through Monday, a total of four days in the mountains. Base camp would be at Mirror Lake, six miles in via the East Lostine trail; our principal goal would be Eagle Cap, a 9,600-foot mountain just south of the lake. Getting to the lake and climbing the mountain would take two days. A third day would be required to get back out. That left one day relatively free; Bob wanted to use it to explore the Lake Basin, a 2,000-acre hole in the mountains stretching north and east from Mirror across the heads of three canyons and containing—along with the headwaters of two of the three largest rivers in the Wallowas—eight major lakes and at least ten smaller ones. I was a little unhappy that we weren't planning to use this day to climb something else, but Bob's use of the word *explore* won me over. That sounded exciting. We would do it his way. My father agreed to provide transportation to the trailhead; now all there was to do was wait.

At the last moment, we added a fourth member to the party. Ron Wolff was from Lewiston, Idaho; Cliff and I had met him at Whitman, where the three of us had plans to pool our resources and rent the upper story of an old house near campus for our sophomore year. Ron was a six-foot, slightly round-shouldered, some-what sardonic paleontology student. He was involved in the local pea harvest, but he could get out of it for a few days. Could we borrow a pack for him? I checked with Bob. We could.

All systems were go. There was no turning back now.

Cliff came to Pullman by rail, arriving late in the afternoon of the day before the trip; I drove down to the depot, anxious and eager, to meet him. He swung off the train, resplendent in red flannel shirt, worn black wool trousers, and scuffed climbing boots, a battered and much-traveled Trapper Nelson packboard his only luggage. Magnificent! The station platform among the wheat fields was instantly transformed into Zermatt. I leaped forward, Richard Halliburton right beside me, to shake his hand.

At dinner that night with my family there was a brief moment of merriment, quite unexpected, when I bragged casually that I ought to have no trouble at all with this trip since according to my calculations I should be able to do forty-five miles a day with full pack and Bob's itinerary only called for six. Cliff, sitting beside me, hooted. "If that's the case," he said, "Maybe you should carry my pack, too. That way I'll have half a chance of keeping up with you." I joined in the general laughter, but I was faintly mystified by it. I knew from my walks about town that I could do four and a half miles an hour for long periods without getting tired; figure eleven hours of walking a day times four and a half miles an hour, and you get fifty miles. Forty-five miles should therefore be a conservative estimate. What was so funny about that?

We went over to Bob's house to bring back the pack I was to borrow from the Lawrences; Cliff had agreed to help me load it. In Bob's tiny dormered bedroom I introduced the two experienced members of the party to each other and watched while they warily sized each other up. The darkness outside the small-paned window turned alpine; the Matterhorn sprouted out of the wheat. Or maybe it was Everest, and Mallory was meeting Irvine for the first time. Once more the ghost of Richard Halliburton seemed to be looking over my shoulder. Bob showed us some pictures he had taken of Eagle Cap. It was an impressive mountain, rounded and bulbous on the south and west but precipitous on the north, dropping through cliff and snowfield and hanging garden and more cliff, two thousand awesome feet straight down into the deep, cold-looking waters of the lake where we would camp. It was that side we would go up. I could hardly wait to get started. Cliff and I took the pack home, loaded it, bragged a little to each other about what we would do on Eagle Cap. We went to bed. The next day would come very early; but, as soon as it might come, I was certain by now that it could not possibly come soon enough.

It did, though. We were up that next morning by five, had Bob in the car and were on our way out of town by five-thirty. An hour later we were leaving Lewiston with Ron safely on board. We climbed out of the Snake Canyon at Asotin, crossed the wheat-heavy Anatone Plateau, snaked into the canyon of the Grande Ronde and back out again. Then came mile after mile of flat timbered country through which the highway bored a corridor as straight as a dead cow's tail and every bit as attractive. Hours passed—real, literal, 60-minute, 3,600-second hours. The tires hummed on the rough asphalt. Tree trunks crept up and flashed past. Where oh where were the mountains?

There they were. . . .

We saw them first as bits and pieces, tiny chunks of gray rock and white snow etched against segments of sky and serrated between the treetops, distant and unbelievable on the morning air. Slowly we drew nearer; the bits and pieces grew and clumped together. They were a frieze; they were a rampart; they were mountains, tumbled and arctic and huge. Sunlight dazzled from a thousand snowfields in a hundred cirques; granite summits glinted with promises. Nearer yet, and nearer. The great arms of the peaks came down and enfolded us; we plunged in among them, beside a leaping river. Buttresses of flying rock jumped skyward from the dry timber. Waterfalls cascaded down stony hillsides. Gravel rattled against the underbelly of the car. The mountains towered.

Deep in the Lostine Canyon, eighteen miles from the town of Lostine, the road finally ended in a wide, dusty parking circle called Two Pan Camp. We heaved the packs out of the car, weighed them, made some last-minute adjustments in the loads. Cliff lifted my pack and held it while I slipped my arms through the straps and buckled the waistband. Then he let go. The weight bore down on my shoulders. It was an oddly comfortable sensation. Bob passed out trail cups, envelopes of heavy polyethylene that would fold flat into a shirt pocket or bulge open to receive water. The last strap was tightened, the last buckle fastened, the last bulge shaken down to a more comfortable position. *Ready?* Ready.

We started. I was a mountain climber at last.

In my sleeping bag that evening, lying between cliff and black water on a small granite toe stuck out from the mountain into the south side of Mirror Lake, I found the details of the day parading through my head in a disorganized jumble of bits and pieces, leaping like confetti, belying the essential simplicity of an experience that outwardly had been nothing more complicated than a six-mile walk up a canyon with a lump of something heavy on my back. Inwardly, of course, it had been something else again. It had been a day of discoveries, a day of revelations and of new experiences, some of which I had expected, most of which had crept up on me unawares. There was, for instance, the matter of mountain distance. I had *believed* that brag about forty-five miles a day with full pack, believed it confidently and with all the misplaced passion of total innocence; it was therefore the rudest of rude awakenings when, forty-five minutes and untold hundreds of miles from the trip's beginning, I had come upon Bob Lawrence standing in the trail and pointing to a small sign nailed to a trailside tree. The sign said *1.* My God, were we only a mile in? Then how come my calf muscles felt like worn-out rubber bands? Succeeding miles were no easier, and by the time I dragged myself up the fifty-foot rise from the long, level upper canyon to the granite rim of Mirror Lake I was literally tottering, my knees shaking with each forced step. Why couldn't they put a road in here? Why did they make us *walk* so far? (And yet, afterward—and this, too, was a discovery—how quickly I recovered! Fifteen minutes of rest on that small, rocky peninsula we called "camp" and I was running casually up talus to a tiny ooze of a spring a hundred feet above us and feeling only slightly winded when I got back down with my aluminum pint bucket filled with sweet, thirty-two-degree water. It was an enlightening and gratifying sensation. Maybe we didn't need that road after all.)

That was one discovery. But there were others, too: the taste of water from a trail-side spring, and the cold of the snow-born Lostine swirling about my feet where we had to ford it three miles in; the fresh smell and the distance-shrinking clarity of the air; the feel of my heart leaping as we rounded that corner of trail in the upper canyon where the towering, half-dome-shaped bulk of Eagle Cap first bursts into view, and I realized with a start that I was actually about to *climb* that thing; the pleasant sense of self-sufficiency arising from the act of locating and cleaning out a small spring at the base of a rock ten feet below camp, freeing us from dependency on that ooze of water at the top of the talus slope—little things, but in that context altogether remarkable. What discoveries lay ahead, in the three days yet remaining?

The last of the day had long since faded from the sky, but it was not dark; there were a million stars up there, a riotous explosion of sparkling, dancing light points. Another discovery: You never see a sky like that in the city. I lay on my back, absorbing it, listening to the lap-lap of the invisible black lake, watching the dark and ragged outline of tall crags against that splendid sky. For a short time the sheer excitement of just *being* managed to keep me awake; then the weariness of the long day took hold, and I drifted off, imperceptibly and deliciously, to sleep.

IV

*D*awn. *Dawn in the Wallowas.*

The flannel liner of the sleeping bag was rough against my cheek. It smelled of previous occupants. Beneath it, beneath my side and hip, the ground was hard and cold. I had not slept well.

I pried an eye open and saw Inside of Sleeping Bag. The other eye followed. Cautiously, I stuck my head out—

—And sat up, wide awake, fumbling for my camera. Only after I had found it, opened the case, released the lens and brought it into focus, set the aperture and the shutter speed, framed, and located and pressed the shutter release, did I remember to breathe again. Off there to the east, over the quiet waters of Mirror Lake, the sky was on fire.

High fluffy clouds scudded from horizon to zenith, their puffy tops pale gray, their flat undersides a brilliant, exploding flame orange. The orange was reflected in the lake, blurred and dancing with the tiny, chopping breeze. Between them, floating between two skies, the black bulk of Pete's Point rose beyond the blacker shapes of trees on the far shore. The water doubled them. Black as it was, this band of twinned mountain and twinned trees seemed insubstantial and nearly transparent; it was a blackness full of latent, achingly pure light.

Like all perfect things, the scene was transitory; already the colors were shifting and fading, the flame dissolving into blue. The day was almost upon us. Bob was building a fire; Ron was sitting up and putting on a sweater, his feet still immersed in the warm folds of his bag. Only Cliff still lay without moving. But that would soon change; surely no one could resist this morning for long. I slipped down to the lake's edge and filled my pint bucket, taking unexpected pleasure in the sight of the cold water pouring over the aluminum brim as the container filled. Lake, stone, sky, and distant peaks seemed imbued with a soft, uniform, and utterly pure light. My first full mountain day was about to begin, and the summit of Eagle Cap was calling.

We left camp shortly after breakfast, moving eastward along the rocky south shore of Mirror Lake. Eagle Cap has a trail up it, but we had no intention of going that way. Bob, who knew the mountain, had made our plans for us: up the cliffs behind the lake, through the pretty little basin at the foot of the North Face, bear east through a high *col* on the mountain's left shoulder, contour south above Glacier Lake, and climb an easy snow slope to the south ridge. Once on the ridge we could stroll to the top. The route was simple, direct, and adventurous, all of which appealed strongly to us. It also contained one tiny but very important flaw. We had no way of knowing it at the time, but the day was going to turn out to be much more exciting than any of us had originally planned.

A gap in the cliffs appeared. A waterfall came pouring through it, but there would be room for us beside the waterfall. Ron said good-bye—he was going fossil hunting; he was not interested in mountaintops. He went off along the lake. The rest of us turned our backs to the water and began scrambling.

It was easy to climb beside the waterfall. It was also convenient—climbing is thirsty work, and here there was always water, never more than ten feet away. We stopped often to take advantage of that fact. (I have many times, in later years, been called a "waterhole-to-waterhole" hiker because I seldom carry a canteen, preferring to depend on the mountains to supply my water. That preference, it is safe to say, stems directly from this waterfall scramble on Eagle Cap. Canteen water is water; waterfall water is earth juice, a much more satisfying beverage. It is a difference worth noting. Where can you find waterfall water in the city?)

At the top of the cliff, fifty feet or so of grassy slope between low stony banks brought us suddenly to a wide, wet, slightly concave meadow beneath the high and shadowed summit cliffs of the mountain. An irregular pond of perhaps an acre lay gleaming in the center of the meadow. Great chunks of white stone were scattered about; interbraided rivulets trickled and gushed into the pond, fed by a broad, sickle-shaped snowfield that sprawled like an unbuttoned Eton collar across the base of the cliffs. The snowfield extended almost to the pass Bob planned to cross. Climbing above the pond, we ventured onto it. Grapefruit-size rocks, released from the rotton cliffs by frost-wedging, whistled past us. Geology in action. We did not linger.

Up to this point, we had been following Bob's plan pretty much as made, without serious mishap. But now a couple of surprises were about to hit us that would amend things somewhat. The first of these was evident as soon as we crossed the pass and got a good look at the southern sky. The weather was turning on us.

We had been climbing all morning in sunshine. A few high clouds had been drifting about, but we had paid little attention to them; it was the sunshine that counted. But we had only seen half the sky; the mountain hid the other half. Now the mountain was no longer in the way, and what we saw was ominous.

Gray clouds. Gray peaks, swirled about with mist. Gray air beyond the clouds, and streamers of gray rain falling. Gray crags at our feet, plunging into gloomy water. Glacier Lake was gray. Even the snow was gray, the snow we had intended to climb and that now provided us with our second surprise.

There wasn't enough of it. And what there was was too steep for safe climbing. To proceed the way we had planned would require ropes and ice axes. We had fifty feet of cotton twine and a geologist's hammer.

Today, faced with that situation, I would retreat. Discretion would prove the better part of valor. There is, after all, another side to Eagle Cap, a side with a trail up it. The wise course would have been to return to the basin at the foot of the North Face, to climb out of it on the west as we had earlier climbed out on the east, to join the trail on the west side, and to proceed to the summit from there. Or alternatively, given the unsettled quality of the weather, perhaps we should have retreated all the way to the safety of camp, to try again, via the trail, the next day.

We were aged, respectively, nineteen, eighteen, and seventeen. We did not choose the wise course. I don't even recall that it entered into the conversation. We were here to climb a mountain, and the question was not how to do it wisely but how to do it expediently, rapidly, and without the ignominy of even a partial retreat. Our plans weren't inflexible; they could be changed, but only insofar as the amendment did not require even a single step backward over the way we had come.

We gathered for a small conference. Bob held out for trying the snow anyway, but much further south than he had originally planned. Down there, at the low point of the ridge connecting Eagle Cap to Glacier Mountain, the slope ameliorated somewhat; and there was a runout at the bottom, meaning we wouldn't be hurled over the precipice into Glacier Lake should we chance to slip. But getting there would still involve crossing wide stretches of snowfield that *did* end in precipices, and neither Cliff nor I liked the looks of that. Anyway, it was too far out of the way. We held the majority vote. The snow was abandoned. We would go *our* way, instead.

Straight up.

We gazed at the eastern face of the mountain. It gazed back at us, three hundred feet of steep talus topped by a one-hundred-and-fifty-foot cliff. Well, the rest of the day was going to be interesting, no matter what else it was. Step right up, folks—watch the mountain climbers in action.

Fifteen minutes of rapid scrambling brought us to the head of the talus slope. The cliff loomed, its hard, knobby granite offering a thousand possible routes. Which to choose? Cliff and Bob had a short argument, which I stayed out of. Cliff ended the discussion by simply starting to climb. His way led up a shallow chimney where a prominent rib thrust out from the main wall. Fifty feet up was a substantial ledge. Cliff sat down on it. "Next," he called.

Next was me. I went.

It was easy. Big, prominent, solid holds, just like the rungs of a ladder. Mountain climbing was a cinch. The ledge with Cliff on it approached rapidly; I hoisted myself up beside him and grinned.

He grinned back. "Just don't look down, old boy," he said. Of course, after a statement like that, I *had* to look. There was Bob, clinging to the face like a gigantic beetle as he scuttled toward us, and far, far below him the gunmetal-gray surface of the lake. I gulped and looked away. "What's next?" I asked.

"That," said Cliff, pointing.

"That" was a smooth-surfaced little rib about thirty feet long leading from our ledge to the next prominent break in the face. It was light colored and about ten degrees short of being perfectly vertical, and I couldn't see a blessed hold on the silly thing. Still, Cliff knew more about these things than I did. I said nothing.

Bob joined us. Cliff rose and approached the rib. I was still wondering how he was going to handle the lack of holds when it suddenly became apparent that he was simply going to ignore it. He straddled the rib and began to shinny. It was a fluid, continuous, easy motion, and it was a beautiful thing to watch. He disappeared over the edge of the upper ledge.

Now it was my turn.

Shakily I approached the rib, laid a hand on it. The smooth toughness of its surface was reassuring. I straddled it, felt the pressure of it against me from chest to scrotum. I began to climb.

Tiny holds seemed to blossom beneath my fingers; my feet found knobs I couldn't see. Slowly, I eased upward. Twenty feet separated me from the upper ledge, then ten. Eight.

And suddenly I could go no further.

The last three feet of the rib were too broad to shinny. The tiny holds I had been using had petered out. My left foot was securely wedged onto a solid four-inch knob, but my right foot clawed featureless granite above a hundred feet of nothing. What in the hell did Cliff do here? I scratched my head—figuratively, because I was afraid to let go even for a second—and thought. Nothing to the left. To the right, then, and slightly upward. Slowly I began to move toward holds less seen than taken on faith. Cliff had made it; they *had* to be there. Six inches, and a long pause. Another six inches—

"The belt," said a voice above me. Cliff had taken off his belt, wrapped it around his right wrist, and, with his left hand and foot securely anchored, was dangling it down to me. It hung six inches from my nose. I grabbed it with my left hand. Cliff pulled. My feet found nonexistent holds; my right hand scrabbled in the sand on the edge of the ledge, found something solid, and hung on. For god's sake, belt, don't break. Footholds—where the hell are the footholds? Help!

I was up.

Knees shaking, I moved to the very back of the ledge. There was a small tree growing there. I snuggled in beside it, next to the granite wall, and waited for the world to stop spinning. Mountain climbing wasn't so much of a cinch after all.

Bob came up rapidly. Cliff offered him the belt, but he waved it aside, vaulting almost jauntily up beside us. He smiled his Teddy Roosevelt smile. Which way from here?

"I don't know," said Cliff.

Help! I thought.

Standing at the front of the ledge, Cliff and Bob had another short discussion. Crouched at the rear of the ledge, I tried tentatively to enter it and was ignored, properly so, since the only merit to my suggestions was that they all led upward from *back here* and I wouldn't have to get up next to that drop-off again. This time, at least, there was no argument. A short distance southward across the face was a large, flat ledge, two feet broad and at least twenty feet long, thrust straight out from the mountain like a causeway to nowhere. It might prove to be just that, of course, but it still seemed to be worth investigating. At least, Bob and Cliff agreed, it would let us get back from the face a way. Perhaps we could gain some perspective on ways to proceed.

There was, however, a problem. The problem was a large flake of stone at the outside corner of our ledge that was blocking all view of the terrain between us and the "causeway." It was only a foot thick, but it was ten feet tall. At the base of its leading edge was a tiny, slanting ledge. The flake overhung it.

Cliff picked up some sand and rubbed it on his hands to remove all traces of oil and moisture. He stepped to the corner of our ledge. Reaching around the flake, he put his right foot on that tiny shelf at its base, and with the friction of his palms pressing in on the rock from opposite sides his only apparent hold, swung out and around, over the long void. His left foot groped behind the rock, out of sight. He disappeared.

Bob and I waited.

From someplace on the far side of the flake Cliff's voice floated back to us: "Oh, nothing *to* it!" He sounded slightly disappointed. What had he found over there? Well, I would have to go see. I stood up and was surprised to find that my knees no longer shook. Moving to the corner of the ledge, I grasped the rock as I had seen Cliff do, and with only a moment's hesitation—but definitely without looking down—I too swung out and around. Onto a steep, knobby granite slope, a slope full of reassuringly broad bumps and hollows, a slope with no continuous ledges but with so many great big lumps on it that it didn't really matter. After what we'd been through, it looked like the King's Highway.

Bob quickly joined us, and we practically ran across to the "causeway."

And now there were no further difficulties—fortunately, for it was starting, at last, to rain. A steep scree slope above the causeway led directly to the mountain's broad summit plateau. We finished the climb abreast, running up the sandy, nearly level ground of the plateau to its highest point, right at the edge of the thousand-foot leap into immensity made by the North Face. There was a big wooden sign there, nailed to a four-by-four post five feet high:

EAGLE CAP
El. 9,595

What a hell of a way, I thought, to finish a climb. It looked like a goddamn street corner.

We entered our names in the jam-packed summit long, adding "Up East Face from Glacier Lake." That ought to impress the riff and raff. Photographs were taken in various poses. Bob insisted on dropping over the North Face to a small ledge three or four feet down and having me take his picture there, as if that had been the way we had come up. For my part, I had had quite enough small ledges to last me for the day. I had also had quite enough of this rainy, messed-up, and strictly nonvirgin summit. It was time to go down. I said as much. Bob nodded. Cliff was urinating off the northeast corner of the summit; he nodded, too. Bob and I started off.

The descent was simple and enjoyable. We followed the route we probably should have used on the way up—running down the western slope to the first spot where one of the north-side snowfields reached it, throwing ourselves onto the snow, and cascading happily down to the pond at the head of the waterfall, accompanied by magnificent displays of flashing snow crystals. It was my introduction to the technique of the *glissade*. It was also my introduction to a phenomenon that I have seen many times since but that still amazes and intrigues me—pink snow. A normal-appearing white snowfield will be leaped upon and slid down by a climber; and when he looks back at the twin trails his boots have made, they will have turned an unmistakable pastel pink. "Algae," Bob said when I asked him. *Well, ask a silly question. . . .* (It would be years before I would accept the fact that he was right.)

Back at Mirror Lake the rain had stopped and the sun returned, draping a magnificent double rainbow around the gray shoulders of Pete's Point. The lake reflected it, transforming it into two perfect concentric circles around a double mountain. Ron was nowhere to be seen, but he had been there; our packs and sleeping bags, which we had left carelessly exposed to the elements, were snug and dry under plastic tarps. When he returned from wherever it was he had gone to, he would receive our profound thanks.

The remainder of the day passed quietly. We rigged the plastic tarps into a sleeping shelter, in case the rain should return. A late lunch was disposed of. Bob went off for a solitary explore around the lake; Cliff and I picked out some of the larger hunks of talus in the neighborhood and went bouldering, vying with each other to pick the most impossible routes to the top of each one. The morning's experience had already faded into memory. Night came flawlessly, laden with stars. Under our strictly unnecessary shelter, the four of us slept.

The next day was the Day of the Backwards Mountain. And the fourth day was the trek out.

Back in the early days of the civil rights movement in the South, in the days of the Montgomery, Alabama, bus boycott, someone asked one of the participants in the boycott how she felt about all the walking she was doing. *"My feets is tired,"* she answered, *"but my soul is at rest."* It was a phrase that kept cropping up in my mind as, on that hot August day in 1961, I trudged the last weary miles to the waiting car. My feets was definitely tired, not only tired but badly blistered, so badly that I would spend much of the next few days crawling instead of walking. The unpadded pack straps cut cruelly into my shoulders. The pack was a poor one; it had been badly balanced to begin with, and ten miles of jouncing over rough trails hadn't improved the situation any. Despite these discomforts I felt buoyant, almost floating, inside. I had realized a lifelong ambition. I was an explorer, an adventurer, a mountain climber, a tamer of the wilderness. I had successfully pitted my own body, my own legs and lungs and hammering heart, against thirty miles, two mountains, and a rainstorm. I had seen and felt new country, had it throw obstacles at me, met those obstacles head on, and beaten every one. The Wallowas had become my conquered province.

We were traveling new country now, past new lakes, under new peaks. We had come in by the Lostine; we would go out by the Wallowa. The car had been moved in our absence, my father at the wheel, and it would be there to meet us.

We passed the Backwards Mountain. There was the couloir Cliff and I had descended, the face from which I had rescued the canteen.

We took a last look at Eagle Cap.

We passed Douglas Lake, Lee Lake, Horseshoe Lake. We began the long, sweeping descent into the canyon of the West Fork of the Wallowa. A tall, pyramidal peak loomed to the south: Cusick Mountain. Now *that,* I thought, I've got to climb some day (and four years later, I would). The barren, wasted slopes of Pete's Point rose like a wall before us. What was behind that wall? (A year would pass before I would find out.)

Now, in the canyon, we spread out along the trail, each seeking his own pace. Ron's pace was slow but steady; he moved without resting, and he would be the first one to the car. Bob's pace was rapid and strong, and even with rests—and some trouble with a disintegrating boot—he would be second.

Cliff was resting longer than Bob, but moving just as strongly. I had seen him last at Lee Lake; but now, five miles later—and still three miles from the car—he came striding up behind me. We walked together for a while, long enough for Cliff to be certain that I was all right, that I would make it all the way to the trailhead. Then, "See you there," he called, and increased his speed. The yellow canvas of his ancient Trapper Nelson pack caught a shaft of sun stabbing down through the forest. He was gone.

I was alone.

Somewhere off to my left, the river sang.

My feet ached in their borrowed boots.

A small doe leaped suddenly from a right-hand thicket, landing on the trail less than twenty feet in front of me. We stared at each other for one eternal moment; then she was gone, back into the brush from which she had come. The mountain swallowed her into silence.

Before me, the trail curved; beyond the curve, filling the middle distance, the broad blue sheet of Wallowa Lake lay like a delft plate caught between two stones. Wallowa Lake meant cars and people and a return to civilization. The trip was over. Surprisingly, perhaps, I felt little regret.

It was the end of the trip. But the trip was only a beginning. The Wallowas were there and could be returned to. And would be.

Understanding

I

The Wallowas would still be there because, on October 7, 1940, the secretary of agriculture of the United States had signed a document commanding it to be so.

That is an oversimplification. Obtaining "Wilderness" classification is never an easy process, and it is impossible to tell how many man-hours of work were logged by citizens and by concerned members of the Forest Service staff, both in Oregon and in the office of the secretary, before the Eagle Cap Wilderness could be proclaimed. But the critical step was that signature. Two seconds of scratching, a line of squiggles made by a fountain pen in the hand of a bureaucrat sitting at a desk in Washington, D.C., nearly three thousand miles away, and the Wallowas were safe forever.

Most of them, that is.

A line is drawn on a map, a proclamation made: Within this line, the land shall remain forever wild. No motors shall cross this line, no buildings shall be built within it, no timber harvested. The only sign of human passage shall be trails. The natural succession of plants and animals shall be maintained, the natural community shall be allowed to function unhindered by human activities. This shall be a place for recreation, for getting close to the land, for feeling it as the first explorers felt it. It shall also be a place where biologists and geologists and ecologists and all those whose study is made of the Earth shall be able to come as to a great natural laboratory, where they may examine the intricate processes and adjustments in processes that form the basic operating capital of this planet and its inhabitants. Here shall watersheds be protected so that the rivers that issue from them may flow sweet and clear; here shall animal habitat be protected, so that the animals who use it may flourish and the Earth may be assured of a continuance of genetic diversity. Within this line is wildernes,.

Unfortunately, within that line may also be small pieces of something else.

The Eagle Cap Wilderness, as it was originally constituted, contained 220,416 acres of land, or precisely 344.4 square miles. Most of this—better than 99 percent of it—was and is federal land. On this land, the secretary of agriculture's proclamation could reasonably be expected to mean something. But the remainder is private land, and for it the proclamation was essentially meaningless.

There is not very much of this private land—perhaps six hundred acres in all, in four parcels. These parcels are widely scattered. Two of them—one on Cornucopia Peak, the other on the west slope of the Hurricane Divide—are largely peripheral, and their presence has little or no effect upon the management of the wilderness as a whole. A third is central and potentially important; it straddles Hawkins Pass, the principal trail crossing between the Imnaha and Wallowa River basins, and its development could affect all travelers, human and otherwise, who take this route. At present, however, it remains undeveloped.

The fourth inholding is also central, and it *has* been developed. This development does not amount to a great deal—a small store on the south shore of Aneroid Lake, a couple of cabins, a fenced pasture for horses. Minor changes, inconspicuous and in harmony with their surroundings. Certainly Aneroid Lake and the East Fork of the Wallowa River should not be withdrawn from wilderness designation because of them. *But—*

We were somewhere on the highest reaches of Pete's Point, climbing upward. Far below us, the round blue eye of Jewett Lake lay on its back and gazed quietly at the sky, a sky that was like a great blue cup inverted over us, its apex directly over the mountain, its rim just touching the distant, miniscule horizon. The slope was steep shale, which chimed musically underfoot at each step; to our left a large snowfield lay beneath black brooding cliffs topped by the blunt summit—or what we took to be the summit—of the mountain. We had long since passed the last tree.

It was my second trip into the Wallowas, and I was not much more experienced than I had been the first time around, although I thought I was. Fortunately, I had more experienced people around me. Bob Lawrence was there; so was his younger brother, Buck, and their father, chemist John Lawrence. A Washington State University entomologist, Bob Harwood, rounded out the party. We had left the Lawrence car beside the powerhouse at Wallowa Lake early on the previous day and started walking, heading south along the East Fork trail. The trail climbed rapidly, switchbacking up the timbered slopes of Bonneville Mountain; soon we were high above the lake, looking down on it through breaks in the trees. Motorboat trails split its surface. The packs felt good on our backs; they were our tickets away from motorboats. We took a long last look at the lake, rounded a corner, and it was gone. Ahead, the trail dipped down to the roaring East Fork of the Wallowa River. I took Bob's picture as he dipped water from a splash pool below a white waterfall. That water came out of the wilderness, and it was good. We had not yet crossed the official boundary of the Eagle Cap Wilderness, of course, but what possible difference could that make?

In less than a mile I had the answer to that question. The trail eased away from the river, rounded a corner, and came back—only it wasn't *river* it came back to. It was reservoir. The white Wallowa had been impounded into dark silence, and half of it was being siphoned off into a pipeline of some sort. There was a small cabin, and there were rails and walkways. The whole thing was so incongruous and so unexpected that it took me a while to connect it with the powerhouse at the trailhead. But that's what it was—a power dam. That pipeline was a penstock, leading two thousand feet down the mountain to a 1,000-kilowatt Pacific Power & Light generator at the bottom. We had been following, not a river, but the ghost of a river, emasculated to drive toasters and dishwashers and electric light bulbs for the citizens of Enterprise and Joseph and Wallowa. I did not begrudge these people their electricity, and certainly there are few ways of generating power that could be less disruptive than a 30-foot-high wooden dam with a long penstock—it's a far, far better way to achieve a two-thousand-foot head than building a two-thousand-foot-high dam would be!—and yet I still felt cheated. Wilderness, to me, meant exploring and pioneering, and one cannot feel like an explorer and a pioneer beside an operating power dam. So it gave me a distinct sense of relief to see a sign beside the trail a few minutes later proclaiming the wilderness boundary. No more nasty dams! Once again I could conquer the wilderness! The great brown-and-white cone of Aneroid Peak loomed above flowers. The trail dipped down to spring after sweet, clear spring. Pack and all, I practically ran through the whispering, bubbling meadows. The Wallowas had become Wallowas again.

Four miles later we hit that store at Aneroid Lake.

Lying in my sleeping bag that night, the black lake lapping a bare yard from my feet, I tried—and failed—to come to grips with that store. We were camped on public land, most of the lakeshore was public land, yet I felt like a trespasser. At a mountain lake, close under high peaks, with all the accoutrements of high peaks— cliffs and bare rock and perpetual snow—I felt as though I were sleeping in somebody's backyard. Or maybe *barnyard* was closer to it. There was horse excrement—no, that is too polite a term, there was horse shit—all around. Horse turds bloomed in the meadows like flowers. It had taken us nearly forty-five minutes to find a place clean enough to camp.

Even so, the worst thing had not been the horse shit or the store or the boats for rent or even the too-rustic, look-at-me atmosphere of the whole thing. The worst thing had been the fence. I was raised to respect fences. Fences were to keep people out, and you respected them because you wanted to keep people out from behind *your* fence. Fences had no place in the wilderness, where the essence of the experience is the freedom to explore, which means the freedom to go anywhere, off trail as well as on, with the barriers imposed by the wilderness itself your only restraint. And yet here we were, high in the wilderness, six trail miles from the car, wilderness-freedom packs on our backs, and we had to cross two fence lines on our way from the trail to our camp. And in order to start our climb of Pete's Point the next morning, we would have to cross them again. It was jarring, it was incongruous, and it was wrong. It was also incontrovertible fact. The store, and the fences, were on private land.

I felt better about things the next morning, there on that headwall above Jewett Lake. The climb so far had not been very exciting, but it had been aesthetically satisfying, very much just what a climb should be. There had been route-finding up steep couloirs, the mountain disappearing behind a lesser cliff brow and then leaping up, overwhelming and gray and magnificent, when we gained the lip. There had been looking down on Jewett Lake, a trailless lake seen from a trailless ridge. There had been leaving the trees behind, entering the world of snowfields and cliffs and vast open slopes of rock. There had been drinking from snowfield runoff (no chance of power dams up here!). Higher yet, on steep shale with the up-and-down world evolving into flatness below, with Aneroid Lake too far away for the fences to be visible, and with the great, steep cone of Aneroid Peak dominating the scene, a genuine mountain feeling had taken hold. The previous year, on Eagle Cap, I had taken that feeling for granted. Now I welcomed it, urging it carefully forward. Down there in the valley, I had lost it twice; up here on the peak, I would not lose it again.

Bob was in front of me, climbing slowly. We were all beginning to tire out. Somewhat self-consciously, I swung into a rhythmic rest-step: step-step-*rest* . . . , step-step-*rest* . . . , a four-beat rhythm with steps on the first two beats and rests on the second two. I had learned the rest-step just that spring on Mt. Hood with Cliff Olin, only there the pattern had been slightly different: *thrust*-step-step-rest, *thrust*-step-step-rest, the *thrust* marking the movement of the ice axe to a new position in the snow. Cliff and I had learned it from a book when we became determined to do spring climbs of Hood and of nearby Mt. St. Helens. We had purchased ice axes and rope for the occasion, along with army surplus crampons and snowshoes and parkas, and we had practiced, in midwinter, by climbing the steep, snow-covered roof of the big old house in Walla Walla that we shared with Ron Wolff, and we had made both climbs. I had not brought my new ice axe to Pete's Point; but now, climbing this endless shale/scree slope, I began to wish I had. Under the north face of the mountain there was snow, sweeping from ridge to lake in one magnificent white gesture, its near edge barely fifty feet south of us. With an ice axe, climbing that snow would be far easier than climbing this shale; without one, climbing it would be foolhardy. One could end up quite rapidly in Jewett Lake. We rested long looks, but nothing else, on the snow.

The gradient began to lessen; the slope was rounding into a ridge. We eased up over the lip of that ridge, walked across its broad, level surface. We came, quite suddenly and unexpectedly, to the smooth edge of time.

Beneath our feet the old world, the world we knew and stood on, fell away; beyond it, on such a scale as to be totally unassimilable, lay depth and silence and distance and utter timelessness. Small breezes moved in the void, carrying out of infinity the sound of falling water. The breezes ruffled our hair. There were gray Eagle Cap, and white Glacier Pass, and Hawkins Pass, and Horton Pass; there was the snow-filled cirque of the Bering Glacier; there were Moccasin Lake and Lee Lake and Mirror Lake and the whole Lake Basin; there was the Backwards Mountain; there were the Matterhorn and Sacajawea and the rugged, unchristened peaks of the blue-gray Hurricane Divide. There, in the far valley, were the town of Joseph and the town of Enterprise and the distant blue perfection of Wallowa Lake. It was a palpable immensity, a feeling of heart-stopping openness. In such surroundings, the titanic ridge on which we stood seemed shrunk to insignificance; only when a small insect began moving a short distance to the north, and I realized with a start that it was John Lawrence, did I have the rude beginning of an outline of a feeling for the true proportions of things.

It was probably a full half hour before anyone thought again of climbing. But then, one by one, we began turning away from the void, turning south, to the tall gray pyramid that loomed there above us. The summit was still calling. Someone—I think it was Bob Harwood—began walking upward along the ridge. The rest of us followed.

We crossed the top end of the great sweep of snow that ended in Jewett Lake; we traversed a sandy saddle. Then we were back on steep shale. But the peak was not far distant. We climbed toward it, our backs to the void. We reached it, but we had been tricked. It was a false summit. Beyond it, beyond a great cirque hung with cornices of snow, a still higher peak lifted itself above us. We could just make out the cairn topping its rounded head.

Well, there was nothing to do but proceed. We dropped down the easy slope to the saddle between the two summits, traversed above the cornices, and climbed the far ridge. We stepped onto the true summit, beside the six-foot cairn that some idiot had built there. Bob Lawrence and I were the last ones to arrive; halfway along we had become fascinated by the cornices, and he had tied into a rope and handed me the other end so that I could belay him as he dropped over the lip with his camera to photograph the underside of one.

We sat on the summit and ate lunch. Besides those huge ridge views, which were still with us, we now had views to the south, of new country, as yet unexplored by any of us. There was the Imnaha drainage, the broad, snow-streaked pyramid of Cusick Mountain, and the jagged twin spires of Krag Peak. There was Sentinel Peak and Marble Mountain and the distant bulk of Red Mountain. There was a veritable sea of new peaks and new places. And yet it was not these that held our attention; we still preferred to gaze, most of us, most of the time, at that immense silence hanging above the Lake Basin. I did not know then, and I do not know now, what makes such views. I know it is not strictly size; bigger views, views from Mt. St. Helens and Mt. Shasta and from the air, have left me far less moved. Surprise certainly enters into it, the suddenness of distance as you top a ridge or a summit, or come to the edge of a plateau; but suddenness is not enough either. The northside summit views from Mt. Hood have such suddeneness and such size, but they have nowhere near the impact. Few places do. Colin Fletcher's description of the Grand Canyon indicates that it may be one of those places. Most sources seem to indicate that Yosemite's Glacier Point is another. In my own experience, I know of only one other spot, one other panorama, that can compare in impact with the ridge view from Pete's Point, and that is the east-facing view from Jackson Gap in the Siskiyou Mountains of southern Oregon. Only at Pete's Point and at Jackson Gap have I yet experienced that special combination of suddenness and immensity and silence and timelessness that is able immediately to put the rest of the world into its proper tiny perspective.

After a while, we turned from the view and started down.

We did not go down the way we had come up, over the false summit and the ridge and the shaley headwall above Jewett Lake. We turned east instead, or southeast, dropping down the steep South Ridge toward the Imnaha. There was no shale here, only sandy places and short, steep stretches of rock. After perhaps an eighth of a mile and a descent of five hundred feet, we came to the head of a snow slope dropping into the cirque between the two summits. It had a fine runout at the bottom, so down we went, in a rapid, no-holds-barred glissade. Since I had been lamenting the absence of my ice axe, Bob loaned me his geologist's hammer. I lost it halfway down the slope and sped the rest of the way out of control. "Haven't you heard the first mountaineering commandment?" asked Bob, at the bottom. *"Hang onto the axe!"* He had come down on his feet, and was in fine shape. Buck had lost his billfold. John Lawrence resignedly strapped on a pair of instep crampons he had been carrying for just such an emergency and started back up the slope. He found the billfold and the geologist's hammer, but he did not find the one other thing that I had lost, along with my dignity; somewhere on that slope today there remains a soggy, much-battered copy of A. E. Houseman's *A Shropshire Lad.*

In the mountaineer's lexicon, to *contour* means to cross a slope at a constant elevation for long distances. The word derives from the technique's resemblance to the act of drawing contour lines on a topographic map. I was about to be introduced to it. From the base of our snowfield we contoured for nearly three-quarters of a mile, following around the inside of the cirque and along its far wall to a point, level with our starting place, that we could cross over. The crossover led to gentle, snow-streaked slopes above Jewett Lake. We dropped several hundred feet to the water's edge. After running most of the day on canteen water, we found the lake delicious. We drank deeply. The outlet stream provided an avenue to Aneroid Lake, nearly a thousand feet below; soon we would be back with the fences and the horses and the store.

I cast a last look back toward the huge, gray bulk of Pete's Point. I started down.

Several hours later, descending the face of Bonneville Peak toward the waiting car, I found myself in a reflective mood. I had just passed the power dam. Why did it bother me so? Once, man-made things hadn't bothered me; the year before, on the trail to Eagle Cap, I had even wished for a road so that we wouldn't have to walk in so far. I wanted to *climb* mountains, not walk past them. On Mt. Hood that spring, and on Mt. St. Helens, I had still been grateful for the presence of roads; in fact, had there been a snow-free road close enough to Mt. Adams, we would have climbed that, too, and it was only the absence of such a road that kept us from it. A two-acre pond behind an inconspicuous dam made of native materials is certainly far less terrain-disrupting than one of those roads I had so recently desired. What was wrong with having it there? What was wrong with the store? Why, for that matter, had I not wished for a road to Aneroid Lake?

Let's start with that last question, I mused, and admit we really don't know. Part of the reason, surely, had to revolve around my superior physical condition this time. On the Mirror Lake trail I had been dragging after a mile; on this Aneroid Trail of equal length and similar character I had gone the full distance with no more than moderate difficulty. I had found I didn't need a road, and that was at least partially responsible for the fact that I didn't want one. But that couldn't be all. I didn't need a road from home to the grocery store, either, but I was grateful for the existence of one. I would not be grateful here.

Of course, I wasn't *exploring* when I went to the grocery store. Here in the Wallowas, the explorer, the pioneer, the wilderness-conqueror in me was close to the surface, and to run across something like a dam or a store meant that someone had conquered before me. That feeling, in fact, had been the one that had immediately leaped up in me and been knocked for a loop back when I had first come upon the reservoir. Was that it? Was *that* why I no longer wanted a road into the Wallowas?

No, that reason didn't hold water, either. I had always wanted to be an explorer, but I hadn't always minded roads. On our bicycles near Walla Walla, Cliff and I had explored many roads. These had been real explorations, full of curiosity about what was around the next bend. They had also been conquests, especially those with large hills on them. You could be an explorer and a conqueror on a road; the thing was possible. You couldn't be a pioneer, but could you be one any better on a well-worn, high-standard trail? The question answered itself. Of course you couldn't. And that, unfortunately, left me right back where I had started.

Well, then, try another tack. Along with "No Pioneering!" the reservoir and the store and the fences had thrown up another message to me, a message spelled out in large, brilliant, almost material neon letters. That message was *incongruity!* Was it the incongruity of these man-made things that made them so disturbing?

And suddenly, thinking back to the morning and the ridge and the deep, timeless immensity seen from the ridge, I knew that I must have found the answer.

I had seen, from Pete's Point, untouched country, vast and open and whole, just as it came from the hand of God. I had seen, at Aneroid Lake and at the power dam, how human presence changes things. These were small changes, still in harmony with their environment—but the East Fork valley was in no way "wild" because I had seen these things. It had lost its wholeness. Only beyond, on the mountain itself, did the wilderness thrill come.

But this answer raised still larger questions. What was this "wholeness" that was missing? Why did the works of human beings destroy it? And why was it so important, especially to a person like me, whose principal reason for going among mountains was to get to the top of one of them? Was it merely a matter of how I *felt* along the trail? If so, what right did I have to resent the power dam? What right did I have to place such vague and egocentric *feelings* above the need of the Wallowa Valley for electric power?

I couldn't answer these questions, and it was easy to realize that I couldn't. But at least I could begin looking for the answers.

From somewhere close ahead came a great water roar. It was the sound made by the outwash from the powerplant generators, a smooth round bore of white water three feet in diameter that jutted straight out for at least fifteen feet in a strictly horizontal direction before finally losing enough momentum to begin to curve downward. My first sight of that outwash, the day before, had left me highly impressed: How on earth, I thought, does that water have so much power left after turning the turbines? Now, knowing the answer to that question, I was somewhat less impressed. Somewhat, but not much. It was still an awesome sound.

The car appeared; the trip was over. I would go home, and I would write a long letter to Cliff—in summer school at the University of Washington—stressing the exciting, he-man aspects of the climb. But it would not be the exciting, he-man aspects that would linger in my mind. It would be the questions—the unanswerable, nagging questions.

II

I made one more trip with the Lawrences that summer. We did not go to the Wallowas but to Goat Rocks, a high, isolated subrange of the Washington Cascades just west of the city of Yakima. We camped by the car at Chambers Lake and made a long day trip into the rocks the next day, four miles by feeder trail to Snowgrass Flat and a further two miles by way of the Cascade Crest route to Cispus Basin, a lovely green cirque full of waterfalls and wildflowers and lingering snow at the base of a ragged, black, strikingly dissected massif called the Pinnacles. We climbed into the Pinnacles. It had been our intention to ascend Mt. Curtis Gilbert, but the approach had been foggy and our written directions foggier still; we ended up, after a harrowing cliff-face excursion that I would prefer to forget, in a small col between the Citadel and Black Thumb in the heart of the Pinnacles, the Conrad Glacier staring blankly up at us from the bottom of a cliff that was so steep it seemed overhung. We retreated without a summit. It was the first time, in my short mountaineering experience, that this had happened, and I found myself—despite Pete's Point—wishing once more for a road. If there had been a road into Cispus Basin we could have saved six miles of walking, and there would have been time to find the proper route up Curtis Gilbert. My brand-new boots, new since Pete's Point, had been improperly fitted, and by the time we stumbled back out to the car my feet were badly blistered. It was not a pleasant experience with which to end the climbing season.

I went back to Whitman, to the start of my junior year. I joined the Outing Club for the first time and was immediately elected vice-president. That meant I would have to perform. The club day-tripped to Anthony Lakes, in the Blue Mountains, and succeeded in reaching the top of the 8,400-foot Lakes Lookout—by trail, yes, but it was a *summit*. After the Goat Rocks debacle, I felt better. Cliff Olin and I scrambled some granite pinnacles just north of the summit, on the edge of a drop-off high enough, and steep enough, to make us feel like qualified climbers. ("Did you look over that edge?" asked Cliff. "*I* did, and it nearly made me drop my rocks.") We returned to Walla Walla in high spirits, laying plans for the annual Outing Club fall overnight trip.

To Aneroid Lake. In the Wallowas.

The sky above Wallowa Lake was perfect, blue and cold and achingly deep and clear. Yellow tamarack leaped from the gray rock around me. I stood on the side of Bonneville Peak, halfway up into that sky, on my way down; eight hundred feet below me and a mile away the curving, four-mile-long lake lay like a great mirror, reflecting the sky and the green forest and the yellow splashes of tamarack and the beige barrenness of the great East Moraine. I had never seen a large body of water so quiet. I still haven't.

This had been an interesting trip, interesting more for the new ideas and new feelings it had given me than for any superficial excitement that might have been present. Indeed, superficial excitement was the principal thing that might have been lacking. The twelve of us—ten students and two faculty advisors—had merely walked six miles up the East Fork valley to Aneroid Lake, spent the night, played around in the snow for a couple of hours, and walked back out. That was all. But in that simple process I had racked up at least five firsts:

It was my first backpacking trip without a climb attached to it. Always before I had gone into the mountains to get to the top of one. This time I was going into the mountains to go into the mountains. The difference may not sound very significant, but it was crucial. Without the blunt urgency of a climb hanging over me, I had been free to observe many things about the mountains, about the trail, and about myself, which had slipped past unnoticed on previous trips. I was trying my hand at "mere backpacking"—and finding it much more interesting than I ever would have thought possible.

It was my first return trip. With the single exception of Kamiak Butte, all of my previous outdoor experiences had involved the exploration of new places. This trip was a return, in its entirety, to territory already covered less than four months before. I was observing two different faces of the same place, instead of two different places, and a whole host of pregnant comparisons arose that had been impossible to see before.

It was the first trip where I used no borrowed equipment. I had purchased a new aluminum-frame backpack less than a month before. My boots had been worked over by a cobbler, I had experimented with several different combinations of socks, and I no longer got blisters. I was well equipped and self-sufficient. It was a good feeling.

It was the first trip made with an organized group, the first trip without Cliff or the Lawrences, the first trip where many were less experienced than I. I found myself giving, instead of getting, advice. This was a new sensation, and a pleasant one.

And finally, *it was my first trip to the Wallowas in any season but high summer.* We walked over new snow instead of leftover remnants from the previous winter. The days were crisp, the single night freezing. There was not even a thought of swimming in the lake.

The combination of these five factors meant that this trip, though it covered the same terrain as my Pete's Point climb the previous summer, was in no way similar to that earlier excursion. This was apparent almost as soon as we left the cars. Because I was familiar with the ground to be covered, I felt a kinship to it; I fell more easily into the rhythms of the trail. Because I recognized landmarks and proportions, there was no need to guess distances, and I was able to pace myself far more efficiently. At the cars, I helped the beginners load their packs for proper balance; once on the trail, I was able to pass out several pieces of advice, such as how to step over water bars instead of on them, and how to rest without taking off your pack, and how much water not to drink in order to keep your body from becoming sluggish and lethargic. I'm sure I got quite carried away with this new ability and made a damned nuisance of myself. Probably. But it didn't matter; I would learn moderation in time, and giving this advice, whether or not it helped the advisees, was helping *me* a great deal.

The trail was crisp underfoot, the air shirtsleeve-brisk. Walking under that sun, in that freshness, was a pure, animal pleasure. We had lunch halfway along the upper valley, near a small *felsenmeer*, a low-angled talus slope without a cliff at the head of it. I judged that partway up the felsenmeer would provide a good view of Aneroid Mountain, scrambled to the spot with my camera, and proved correct. Curiously enough, I felt no pride, only a growing sense of familiarity, of *at-home-ness*, with the wild country around me. On my first trip into the Wallowas I had felt that sensation briefly as Cliff and I returned toward camp from the Backwards Mountain; now I felt it almost constantly, growing stronger with each step.

Near Aneroid Lake, the trail disappeared under fresh snowbanks one and two feet deep. As the only one in the party who had been over the trail before, I took the lead. Soon, wide silver water appeared beyond ragged trailside trees. Remembering the store, I cut away from the trail, down and to the right, to a large flat at the north end of the lake. The group followed. The developments were directly opposite, but invisible. Pete's Point hung over the lake like a great white cloud. We pitched camp.

Morning dawned clear and cold and utterly still. The mirror-calm lake was full of the mountain. I was out of my sleeping bag almost as soon as it was light, racing up the westward slope away from the lake to meet the downward-sweeping arc of the sun. I had not slept particularly well. Somewhere, in some book, I had once read that a packboard makes a good mattress. It doesn't. I ached all over.

After breakfast, I announced that I was going up to look at Jewett Lake, and would anybody like to come along? Two girls named Gretchen and Donna accepted my invitation. We walked southward along the west shore of the lake, past my July campsite, through the pasture area where the horses had been grazing. The horses were gone, and the fence was down for the winter. I felt a great and glorious relief at being able to move over that ground unbound by fences, and the relief found its way into song: "Ohhhh, Freedom! Ohhhh, Freedom! Ohhhh, Freedom over me. . . ."

The girls looked at me and shook their heads. We walked up the curving, snow-choked couloir that in the summer had held the outlet stream of Jewett Lake. Toward the top the way became very steep; I took the lead with my ice axe, chopping steps in the wind-packed snow. We climbed into a vast white treeless silence under the great snow-covered wall of the mountain. Jewett Lake was frozen over; we linked arms and skated across. I climbed a little way up the skirts of Pete's Point, just far enough to be able to slide back down. The sun highlighted our summer's route up the cirque wall; I thought briefly of climbing up into that sweeping ridgetop view, but brushed the thought from my mind. It was ten-thirty. We had promised to be back by lunch.

Sun on snow crystals made dazzling haloes around us as we glissaded back toward camp.

Dusk had come by the time we got back to the cars, and the sky was a fading red behind the black bulk of Joseph Mountain. I walked up the parking lot for one final look at the powerhouse. It was roaring away in the gloom, the thick, powerful bore of water exiting from the turbine pale and ghostly against the vague outline of the building. The questions from last summer were welling up in me once more. This building and this thundering stream of white power represented a need—the need for the people of the Wallowa Valley to have electricity. In fulfilling that need it was impinging, to a mild degree, on my enjoyment. But what right did I have to resent that? Even though I had learned, on this trip, that a hike could be enjoyable in itself alone—and not simply as the prelude to a climb—I had no answer to that. It was still my *enjoyment* against others' *need*, and enjoyment would have to come out second best. Unless, that is, I could do one of two things:

• Unless I could prove that there was a need for the type of enjoyment a reservoir interrupts, a need greater than the Wallowa Valley's need for an extra thousand kilowatts of electricity.

• Or, alternatively, unless I could prove that there was a need for untouched mountains that went *beyond enjoyment;* a need that made human enjoyment irrelevant, or at best only a symptom of that need's fulfillment; a need *of the mountains themselves* to remain undeveloped.

And I could prove neither of these things. Not yet, anyway. I turned back toward the cars.

Eventually, I would come to feel that this trip was a turning point, that this first return trip, this first trip-without-a-climb, would mark also my first tentative touch with the deep rhythms of the living wilderness. I felt none of this yet. I merely felt tired. I crawled into the back seat of the old Ford sedan belonging to Conrad White, the principal Outing Club advisor. Another hiker was already there, a girl named Melody. The car spun along the quiet black waters of Wallowa Lake, past a shifting kaleidoscope of peaks and dull red sky. I named each peak aloud, but more for myself than for Melody or Conrad. Then the mountains were behind us and we were traveling into black night. We sang songs, the two of us in the back seat providing most of the voice. The car sped toward Walla Walla. Behind it, out of sight but vividly present, ragged white peaks lifted themselves out of ebony silence toward a sliver of moon. Someday, far in the future and in another town, Melody and I would be married.

The days quickly settled back into their routine form. I went to classes, came home from classes, went again. Winter came on, Walla Walla winter, cold and wet and miserable. I dreamed of sunlit summits. Cliff Olin and I were no longer rooming together, but we met often; and each time we talked, the subject was mountains. Gradually, out of the tedium of classes, a plan began to emerge—a sweeping plan, a grandoise plan, a plan such as only a pair of bored, mountain-struck college students could have conceived. We would take our packs, our sleeping bags and tents, our ice axes, crampons, snowshoes, and ropes, and the entire nine days of spring vacation, and disappear into the Wallowas. Entering by way of the great U-shaped gate of Hurricane Canyon, we would make winter ascents of four peaks, including the two highest in the range: 10,000-foot Sacajawea and the Matterhorn, 9,700-foot Twin Peaks, and 9,200-foot Sawtooth. Christmas came, and January, and February. We recruited a third climber, a twenty-seven-year-old Whitman music instructor named Bob Zimmerman, whose previous experience consisted of a single ascent of Long's Peak in the Colorado Rockies. (No matter: He was willing, and we were confident, and he had a car to get us there.) February turned to March; the margins of my class notes began sprouting sketches of mountains. Maps covered my floor, becoming a mishmash of pencil marks. *There* would be a good spot for a high camp . . . *there* was a steep slope that might avalanche . . . *there,* or *there,* looked like a possible summit route. . . . Slowly, the itinerary became settled. Saturday we would pack in to the base of Sacajawea; Sunday we would climb up and over the summit, carrying the packs, to camp in the high col between Sacajawea and the Matterhorn; Monday we would climb the Matterhorn. Tuesday we would take a break, lounging about and enjoying the pleasures of a winter camp above timberline (Bob planned to take cigars). Wednesday would be moving day, back to the floor of Hurricane Canyon and up the far side to Legore Lake, between Twin Peaks and Sawtooth; Thursday would be reserved for one of those two peaks, Friday for the other. On Saturday we would go out. That gave us one extra day for possible miscalculations of time, stray blizzards, accidents, anything else that might delay us; we figured the one day should be sufficient. March crept past. We told our plans to Outing Club advisor Conrad White. "Forget it," he said. "You'll never make it." Such sound advice was quite properly ignored. After all, we were Experienced Mountain Climbers. The last week of classes came and slowly ticked away. Monday, Tuesday, Wednesday. . . . . I loaded my pack. Thursday. . . . .

Friday. Now it would come. My last trip into the Wallowas had been less than adventurous, and it had failed to answer my Pete's Point questions. Now I would try the opposite tack. I was set for a superadvanture. Let it arrive.

III

On Friday night I got little or no sleep. This was not due to excitement over the coming adventure but due to pain. For several days I had been nursing a dull sensation in my lower jaw that chose, about suppertime on Friday, to erupt into a full-fledged toothache. The right side of my mouth swelled shut. Aspirin was no help. I went to bed about ten-thirty and for six hours lay tossing and turning in agonized discomfort on my increasingly rumpled bed, waiting for the dawn's early light, or the rocket's red glare, whichever came first. Finally, at four-thirty in the morning, I gave up and got dressed. Bob was due in an hour. I ate a light breakfast, avoiding the right side of my mouth; I tried, without success, to read a magazine; I got out my guitar and, very quietly, so as not to disturb the landlady, played Sor and Carulli and Aguado and Giuliani. Bob arrived, nearly half an hour late. He listened sympathetically while I explained my somewhat haggard and misshapen appearance. "Shall we call the trip off?" he asked. I thought not. The tooth felt better as long as I moved about and kept my mind off it, and anyway, it couldn't last forever, could it? We loaded my pack into the tiny space behind the rear seat of Bob's Volkswagen beetle; the front trunk was already full of his own gear. A stop a block away to pick up Cliff and we were off, wheeling southward through Milton-Freewater and turning left into the Blue Mountains. Wedged into the back seat beside Cliff's familiar Trapper Nelson, I tried once more to sleep. But the tooth was throbbing again.

Under a gray sky, heavy and threatening, we sped eastward.

In Enterprise we frittered away a good half hour trying to locate something stronger than aspirin, or more specifically tooth directed. The clerk in the Rexall store was sympathetic but not very helpful; over-the-counter preparations strong enough to deal with toothache pain simply don't exist. Bob asked about dentists. The clerk mentioned three. One was in Lostine, ten miles back the way we had come. Another was supposed to be very good, but she thought he was a Seventh-Day Adventist and wouldn't work on Saturday. The third was an old man who for many years, until quite recently, had been the only dentist in Wallowa County. His touch was not as sure as it had been, but he still practiced. She thought we might find him in his office, on the second floor of the hotel across the street.

Bob and Cliff went to get coffee. I went resolutely across the street to seek out the dentist.

On the stairs I had a moment of panic. I have always been a prac- ticing dental coward, and the clerk's description of the old man's technique had not been calculated to allay any fears I might feel. Still, the expedition was important, and the tooth was jeopardizing its success. I pressed warily forward, down a musty L-shaped hallway. At its very end was the office I sought. I knocked lightly. There was no answer. I knocked again, more loudly. Still no answer. From the far side of the door came the rhythmic sound of snoring.

I located Bob and Cliff in a nearby café. "That was quick," said Cliff. "He wasn't there," I lied. "Anyway, I'm feeling better." That was another lie, but I desperately did not want to be the cause of the expedition's collapse. I had coffee, too, drinking it carefully through the left side of my mouth. Then we were off, headed for the mountains once more, now only minutes away. Six miles down the road we stopped to register our planned itinerary with the U.S. Forest Service at the district ranger's office in Joseph. Five minutes later we were in Hurricane Canyon.

There is an almost stupefying abruptness about the beginnings of these Wallowa canyons. The north side of the range is formed by a fault scarp almost six thousand feet high. The canyons come down to the edge of this scarp and stop instantaneously, as if chopped off, almost like a cross-sectioned model for use in a geology class. There are roads partway into most of these canyons; in the case of Hurricane, the penetration is a little under two miles. The roads change character almost as suddenly as do the canyons themselves. One moment they are plains roads, straight and level and open; in the next they become mountain roads, twisting above foaming streams, enclosed by trees and by towering walls of smooth, hard stone.

The Hurricane Canyon road was passable all the way to its end at Falls Creek Campground, although the last mile was frosted with an inch or more of fresh snow. We drove to the campground and twenty yards beyond, up a short, steep rise to a tiny parking lot at the trailhead. The parking lot was already occupied by another vehicle, a huge four-wheel-drive rig; we snickered a bit over what the driver of that monster would feel when he came back from wherever he was and found that a lowly Volkswagen had made it just as far as he. The packs came out and were propped against a picnic table while we sorted their contents to distribute the weight evenly among us. Foods that had come from Walla Walla in their grocery store containers were ladled into plastic bags. There was a great deal of mirth as the peanut butter received this treatment; bagged, it had the appearance and consistency of something entirely different and not very polite. All through the remainder of the trip the peanut butter would be handed back and forth to the request, "Pass the shit, please."

At last we were ready. We buckled down the packs and tied our snowshoes onto them; for the time being, at least, there wasn't enough snow to warrant wearing the things. Including the snowshoes, the packs weighed in at over fifty pounds each. But we were only going three miles, and maybe a weight on my back would take my mind off my toothache, which had kicked up to full strength again. The trail stretched before us, clean and white under the trees. We started.

The way dropped quickly to a small stream, passed through a grove of trees, and came out onto a steep open bank high above the spring-swollen thunder of Hurricane Creek. The packs made balance precarious on the snowy trail. We went across slowly, ice axes held ready to arrest a fall. Then there were more trees, and level ground away from the river. Snow began falling in tiny, cold, vision-obscuring flakes. But the outline of the trail was still visible, even in the middle of meadows whose edges had receded into the storm. We kept going. Cliff and Bob were vague shapes seen through a flurrying white curtain. A thin layer of snow was building up on their packs and on their hats. It must be building up on mine, too. We moved slowly, bent into the storm, each watching the ground directly in front of him because if you raised your head to look in any other direction the snow stung into your eyes. I thought, dully: Well, you wanted adventure, didn't you? My tooth was aching abominably. But we were making progress; each step brought us farther from the car and therefore closer to Sacajawea and the Matterhorn and Twin and Sawtooth. Sawtooth. Tooth. Tooth? Nasty word! We moved through an endless string of meadows (where the snow blew and stung) and strips of trees (where the snow drifted and seeped down our necks). In one of the strips, on one of the trees, a sign was nailed: *2.* Cliff raised his ice axe and pointed to it, grinning broadly, snowflakes on his eyebrows. "Mr. White said we'd only make half a mile." He was still moving strongly, as was Bob. I wasn't: The sleepless night and the constant pain were beginning to take their toll. I staggered and lurched. When would it end? The trail came down to Hurricane Creek for the first time since its beginning. Calm water moved between snow-covered banks. Then there was a hill to climb, on the lip of a deep, narrow inner canyon in whose dark depths waterfalls thundered. The snowfall let up. Ahead lay Slick Rock Creek, our proposed first night's camp.

Slick Rock Creek had been chosen, from the map, because it offered both water and proximity to the base of Sacajaweja's North Ridge, the route we planned to take to the summit the next day. Now that we saw it in person, or "in creek," we were less enamored of it. It had no valley. Hurricane Canyon had narrowed to a tiny, abrupt V, the most constricted point on its entire length. At the bottom of the V, filling it, rushed the river, gaining speed as it gathered itself together to plunge, in less than a hundred feet, into the narrow, thundering Inner Gorge. There were bridges of snow, many feet thick, crossing it in several places. The canyon wall on our side was steep and treeless and desolate. It bent slightly, forming a shallow bowl; just at the inside curve of that bowl, whipping down the mountainside in a frothy series of waterfalls, was Slick Rock Creek. New snow lay like a thin frosting over everything.

On a small shelf fifty feet or so above the trail we found room for the two tents, pitched end-to-end. I joined in the pitching of them, but by now I had no intention of sleeping there. Not this night, at any rate. I was going back to Enterprise. The damn tooth was still throbbing, and that constant pain was weakening me, sapping my strength, holding me back. Worse, it was holding Bob and Cliff back. A party is only as strong as its weakest member. To resolutely continue forward, pretending to ignore the pain, was to court defeat—or possibly worse. A pain-benumbed brain is liable to errors in judgment. And errors in judgment are one thing a mountain climber simply cannot afford.

I borrowed twenty dollars and Bob's car keys. I said good-bye to Bob and Cliff. And then, packless, snowshoeless, my ice axe and camera my only burdens, I strode off, alone, down the mountain.

Somewhat to my surprise, I found the walk out to be almost enjoyable. The snowfall had not returned, and the air was fresh smelling and sweet as only recent precipitation can make it. The trail was clear, walking was easy. On either side, the walls of the canyon rose starkly into low-hanging clouds. Without the pack, and with the toothache perversely subsiding, I was moving strongly and easily for the first time that day. There is something spirit-buoying about walking confidently forward, by one's self, in the context of such magnificence. I felt comfortable and free and right.

It took me slightly under an hour to reach the car. There was still plenty of light. I tossed my axe and camera into the back seat, slipped behind the wheel, and, driving a Volkswagen for the first time in my life, chugged off toward Enterprise through three inches of loose, new snow.

In Enterprise I stopped at the first phone booth and rang up the elderly dentist the pharmacy clerk had sent me to that morning. There was no answer: Perhaps he was still snoring. I tried the office of the Adventist, just in case. No answer there, either. I drove the ten miles to Lostine, located a booth there, phoned *that* dentist, office number, then home number. Still no answer. This was getting ridiculous. Back to Enterprise, try the old man once more. Nothing. What was the time I had heard that Adventists considered the Sabbath over? Was it six o'clock? My watch said five-fifty-five. I waited ten minutes, crossed my fingers, and dialed the number listed under "home" for the Adventist. I held my breath. One ring, two, a click; and a calm, warm, competent-sounding masculine voice said, "Hello?"

Fifteen minutes later I was in a dentist's chair, relaxing completely for the first time in more than twenty-four hours, while strong fingers, every bit as competent as the telephone voice had implied, extracted the offending tooth.

"Now, I'm not going to try to tell you not to complete this climb," he said, when the tooth was out, and the fee—a miniscule amount, it seemed to me, for the service rendered—had changed hands. "You're young and strong, and you'll probably come through it all right. But try to take it easy. A toothache is a disease, and an extraction is an operation, and you don't recover immediately, any more than you would from an appendectomy. There's a real possibility that your gum may hemorrhage if you push yourself too hard. Were you going back to your camp tonight?"

I said I didn't know.

"Well, don't. Tell the hotel clerk to put a throwaway cover on your pillow in case you bleed a little. Get a good night's sleep and catch up with your friends in the morning." He handed me a prescription for a powerful pain medication, "Just in case," shrugged off my thanks ("I wouldn't have slept very well, knowing you were in pain"), and showed me to the door. He closed it behind me. I was alone once more. Overhead the night was clearing, and stars were beginning to come out.

I did not go to the hotel.

Perhaps it was the Novocain, or the residual effects of pain and loss of sleep, or the deep relief felt at getting the toothache completely under control at last, and out of the way. Perhaps it was a combination of these factors. Whatever it was, it affected my judgment, and I did not do what I should have done.

I got back in Bob's car.

I turned on the ignition and the headlights.

I drove south, out of town, back toward the mountains—back

toward the black maw of Hurricane Canyon—back toward the road's end, and the trail, and my friends in their precarious canyon-side perch near Slick Rock Creek. The hour was still early, not yet eight o'clock. I had made it the other way, from camp to town, in less than an hour and a half. That meant I should be back in camp by nine-thirty. I could rejoin Bob and Cliff, get a good night's sleep, and be up and about the next morning, on schedule, ready to start climbing Sacajawea.

There was more new snow on the canyon road, covering my outward tracks, and the little car fishtailed a bit as I drove at what must have been reckless speed back toward the parking lot at the trailhead. I remember the headlights stabbing the darkness beside the river, black water foaming thunderously among snow-covered boulders. I remember watching for landmarks, watching the snow deepen, and praying that I could make it all the way. Then I was there: To my left the dim, open shape of the lower parking lot, ahead the last twenty-yard rise to the upper parking lot and the trailhead.

The car would not go up that final rise. Mad, cursing, my blood pressure skyrocketing, I flung machine at mountain again and again, only to have it stall and die each time less than halfway up the slope. The sound of the motor echoed from the canyon walls. The smell of overheated metal began to creep through the heater. But I would not give up; somehow, it seemed terribly important to put the car back *exactly* where Bob had left it. Stall, die; yank on emergency brake; restart; back up and race forward. Stall, die. . . . The cycle was finally broken when, with a particularly vicious yank, I pulled the emergency brake handle out by the roots. Realization as to what I had been doing flooded in on me. I backed the car down one final time, and this time I turned to the left, into the lower parking lot, and found a level spot where the brakeless car wouldn't roll away into the river. I turned off the motor.

Silence flooded in.

I glanced at my watch. It was past ten o'clock. Somehow, more than two hours had slipped by since I had left the dentist's office! Well, I would have to move fast. I picked up my ice axe and camera, locked the car, and started up the white trail.

Clouds had swum back in to cover the few stars; even above

them, there was no moon. It was cave dark under the trees. Clearings were little better. The steep, open bank-traverse above Hurricane Creek near the trailhead had to be done mostly by feel, the river gnashing its teeth unseen below, the trees ahead vague black shapes, only the whiteness directly beneath my feet solid enough to trust. In insulated boots, three layers of wool clothing, Navy-surplus parka, and arctic flying gloves, I was barely warm enough. Yet some urgency drove me forward. Ahead was companionship, ahead was my warm sleeping bag, ahead were summits and getting-the-trip-back-on-schedule. Biting on sterile gauze, trying not to think about hemorrhaging, I strode forward into impossible and frigid blackness.

Then, suddenly, I was no longer walking. I was standing rock still, on tiptoe it seemed, every nerve and every sense awake and alert for the first time since before the toothache had begun, back in Walla Walla. What on earth was that sound?

I was somewhere near the middle of a pale, cold clearing. Mountains were huge vague shapes, the near line of trees a blackness against a blackness. And from somewhere within that vagueness and that blackness had come a scream, a scream like that of a mortally wounded child, loud and piercing and absolutely terrifying.

The onset of panic is not immediate. There is a moment just before when all senses are perfectly attuned, when the mind races with watchlike precision and accuracy. And in that crystalline moment, there in that black-white, icy, uncertain meadow, I recognized that sound and catalogued it: Panther!

Then the panic set in, and I started running.

It lasted only a moment. Within ten feet, I had brought my plunging legs under control and was walking again, somewhat anxiously, but with purpose and direction. The direction was down. The scream of that panther had completed the job the broken emergency brake handle had started: It has cleared the last cobwebs of Novocain and pain shock and sleeplessness from my brain, leaving me fully conscious and rational for the first time in two days. I could see now—it was obvious!—that what I was engaged in was an irrational act, that to attempt to hike, at midnight, alone and unequipped, three miles into rugged, snow-covered mountains with the threat of more snow hanging about them, was folly of the rankest sort. And I was profoundly grateful to that cat, wherever he was, for deciding to shoot his mouth off. For bringing me to my senses at last.

In ten minutes I reached the car and safety.

The remainder of that night passed by in ways that I would just as soon forget. Curled into the back seat of the Volkswagen, I tried to sleep; but the lack of space, the cold creeping insidiously in around the doors, and the residual adrenalin from the panther's scream made sleep impossible. My knees, robbed of a space to straighten out, cramped nastily; my toes numbed; whichever part of me it was—back or arms or legs—that was not directly against the seat cushion felt chilled and extremely uncomfortable. Frost formed on the inside of the windows. From time to time, driven by the cramps and the cold, I would get out of the car and exercise, running up and down the parking lot until I could feel circulation returning. Then I would try once more, and fail once more, to sleep. Time crept, an hour and a half in my mind to each twenty minutes on my watch. Outside, the night remained black.

Then, finally, when I crawled out of the back seat for my umpteen thousandth exercise period, the sky was no longer black but only almost black; trees about the parking lot, unseen previously, were dim silhouettes against it. With agonizing, imperceptible slowness, the almost-black grew lighter. Detail began to creep out. Soon I could see the stream banks, could see the trail, could begin to make out needles on the nearer trees. By six o'clock I judged that it was light enough. I left my prison behind and for the third time in less than twenty-four hours started up the Hurricane Canyon trail.

Moving once more, freed from the confinement of the car and the darkness, I felt the doubts that had crept in during that long night dissolving and disappearing, felt confidence returning. I had made it through the night after all. I had survived the storm. Nature could not knock me down. She had tried and failed. Despite the fatigue of nearly forty-eight hours without sleep, my step was almost buoyant as I moved along the trail. The tricky spot above the river went by with not so much as a fumble. Places that had held unknown dangers in the dark were now just sections of the trail. Soon I would reach the point in the meadow where I had turned around last night. Soon I—

I stopped, the hairs on my neck prickling erect. Here was the clearing I had turned around in. Fifty feet ahead was my far point. My tracks were clear and sharp in the new, already crusted snow. And overlaying them, blurring them, running in the same direction, and obviously made only shortly afterward, was another set of tracks. Paw tracks. Cat-paw tracks. They looked as large as dinner plates.

I stood for a long time, looking at those tracks, tracing their course with my eyes. There they came out of the woods to the left, moving diagonally up the slope to the trail. Here they joined my route and turned sharply southward, going my way, following my tracks, obscuring them. I moved slowly along. Here I had turned around. The cat had kept going. His tracks were alone, now, trotting purposefully along the trail. In a few hundred yards he turned off to the right, slanting upward into the timber. The trail stretched unmarked before me once more.

I was almost sorry to see those tracks diverge. Evidence of the cat was frightening, but it was also, in an odd sort of way, a form of companionship. It was proof that I was not the only living thing in these mountains, and it made them seem less impersonal and less huge. Now I was alone again. I quickened my pace along the trail. Cliff and Bob were up there somewhere, and I needed friends.

By seven-fifteen I was climbing the slope above the Inner Gorge. Above me the sky was clearing to a brilliant, cloud-dotted blue. And somewhere close at hand were Cliff and Bob. But where? Exactly where should I leave the trail? I shouted: *"Helllooo the caammp!"* After the echoes came only silence. I moved another hundred yards up the trail; now I could see Slick Rock Creek. I shouted again. And this time there came an answering call, off to my right: "Up here."

I moved toward the sound. The tents came into view, small and vulnerable on that vast wall. Beside them stood Bob and Cliff, conversing with each other as they prepared breakfast, and the sound of their conversation was like a door pulling down to shut off the silence. They seemed almost to be ignoring me, but even *that* felt good. Let us return to normalness as soon as possible. I climbed up beside them. "Want some breakfast?" asked Bob.

I was home.

IV

An hour later we were moving again.

We did not go up the flank of Sacajawea, and we did not carry the packs. This was to be a reconnaissance trip, a use of the extra day in our schedule, a day for me to recover before the real work began. In fact, as they had planned the foray, Cliff and Bob had assumed that I would stay behind, resting in camp and recouping my strength. I would have none of it. A little food and forty-five minutes of deep, solid sleep in Cliff's tent, its interior sun-warmed to a good sixty or seventy degrees, and I was refreshed and ready to start. I have read, since, that it is not how long you sleep, but how deeply, that determines how rested you will be upon awakening. I believe it. That forty-five minutes had been as good as a full night. I was alert and eager for the day.

The goal that Bob and Cliff had set was to get high enough on the west wall of the canyon to be able to look across and see the full sweep of Sacajawea's west side, so that we might see how good our advanced route-planning had been. Unfortunately, there was no easy way to do this. Above the tents a little way there was a cliff band perhaps a hundred feet high. Any route up the wall was going to have to deal with that cliff band. And we were too close to it to make any real attempt at sensible route-finding. We would have to proceed by guess and by hope.

Our first try got forty or fifty feet up into the cliff band and dead-ended. Holds that had started out big and solid and plentiful grew

increasingly small and crumbly and scarce, finally petering out altogether. Shifting about on a tiny ledge above nothing, looking for a
way to proceed, Cliff rubbed his camera strap against a sharp rock,
severing it and sending the camera careening down the face. We
picked our way down to it. It was battered but still operable. Don't
press your luck. We abandoned that route.

The second try, six or seven hundred feet to the north, was better. Here, on a northern exposure where yesterday's snowfall still
clung, we advanced to within twenty feet of the cliff-top before
things got sticky. That was too close to give up. Off to the left, Cliff
thought he perceived a possible route. Rope coiled around his
shoulder, and with Bob holding his ice axe, camera, and gloves,
Cliff led that way. We advanced another ten feet. Now the principal
hazard was snow, not new snow that you could brush from the
holds but old, compacted stuff with the general consistency—and
coefficient of friction—of ice. Cliff called for his axe. Bob edged up
and handed it to him. Chips flew, dull white at the beginning of
their flight, sparkling as they left the cliff shadow behind and arced
into the sun. A line of clear holds slowly developed. We inched
diagonally upward, over the lip and into the light.

Now there was scree above us, steeply angled, precariously balanced, and streaked with snow. A few stunted trees growing out of
it at odd angles did nothing to improve its appearance. It seemed
too steep for a direct frontal attack. We angled southward up it, our
axes doubling as canes. We rounded a corner. Slick Rock Creek lay
below us; ahead was a substantial snowfield, slanting upward to the
right, its base in the creek several hundred feet below. After the
scree, the snow looked easy. We moved onto it and began kicking
steps.

When you have been in the mountains for a while, you begin to
develop certain expectations about how the terrain will lie, based on
your experience with similar portions of the landscape. One of
these expectations is that the angle of a slope will decrease as it
approaches a crest, making any climb increasingly easier as you approach its top. Lulled by this knowledge, we went confidently forward. But this snow slope was an exception to the rule; instead of
decreasing as we approached the ridge, the angle *increased*, working its way upward into something resembling a wall. This change

was gradual, we were not expecting it, and by the time we noticed it, it was too late. We were committed. The never-ending snow seemed too steep for a safe descent. It was funneling us up into a tiny rock-walled bowl. Unroped, we could not traverse to safer ground without risking a fall. We could only climb carefully upward into the funnel—on snow so steep our bellies almost touched it when we stood in our meticulously carved steps—and hope the rock at its head would offer a way out.

The bowl at the head of the funnel was about twenty feet wide, the rock that formed it thrusting perhaps twelve feet straight up out of the snow. Approaching the right side of this bowl, Bob thrust his ice axe through his belt, found his holds, and swung onto them. He clung to the cliff, moving slowly.

Off to the left, Cliff and I were not faring quite so well. We found no holds, only lumpy-textured red rock. We advanced cautiously. At the extreme apex of the bowl a chimney offered a possible route; near its bottom the snow ended in a level three-foot shelf. I sat on that shelf, safe for the time being, and watched Cliff attempt the chimney. He got four or five feet up into it and dropped down again, breathing hard. "I might be able to do it," he said, "if what was beneath me was level ground. But if you slip here, it's curtains." He indicated the slope we had just come up, sweeping dizzily away for hundreds of feet to end in the foaming waters of the creek. I took one glance downward, clung to the rock, and faced quickly to the right. How was Bob faring?

The cliff was empty. Bob was nowhere to be seen. Had he made it? Or had he slipped, unseen, not crying out, and was he now lying broken in Slick Rock Creek?

Cliff yelled. "Mr. Z!" There was a silence, but it had in it the clink of an ice axe on stone. Then he was safe! But why didn't he answer?

It was my turn to call. I did so. "Mr. Z!" (Almost panicked.) "Where are you?"

Bob's face appeared over the rim to the right. He had been exploring. "It's easy from here," he reported. "Come on up."

Well, you see, there's this little problem. . . .

In ten minutes it was over. Bob had come around to the top of the chimney, lowered himself into it as far as he dared, and waited.

Cliff and I had taken turns throwing the rope until the end of it came close enough for Bob to grab; he had climbed upward a few feet, braced himself, belayed us while we tied onto the rope, and then, one by one, he had hauled us over the rim. We moved a hundred feet across gentle scree to the sunny top of a rock outcrop, sandy and level and broad, and lay down. How good it was to be alive in the midst of such magnificence!

And magnificence it was. We had now reached an altitude of eight thousand feet, more than two thousand feet above our camp near the floor of the canyon. We sat on a point thrust out into airy space from the main mass of the Hurricane Divide. To the west the backbone of the divide sawtoothed southward, sweeping across the scene for miles, a bewildering jumble of black crags and white snow, its lowest summits a thousand feet above us. At its feet, far down, lay the narrow U-shaped gulf of the canyon. (I knew what that U meant; Bob Lawrence had told me. It meant that a glacier had been there once.) Framed in the distant end of it was a sawed-off dome we were easily able to identify as Eagle Cap. And across from us, huge, white, and overpoweringly close, her summit rearing more than two thousand feet above our viewpoint, her base lost in the depths of the canyon, was Sacajawea. The Matterhorn was a black satellite on her southern flank.

Absorbed in the excitement of the climb, we had almost forgotten that this view of Sacajawea had been our primary goal; but now we turned our attention to it. What was the best way up? Was it possible to tell?

We studied the mountain. Sacajawea, from this angle, resembles a gigantic chocolate cupcake covered with white icing, and with a huge bite taken out of one side. *Bite* is, in this case, more than just a visually descriptive term. That hole was made, in the last fraction of an eyewink of geologic time, by a minor feeder glacier that literally chewed its way down through the mountain on its way to join the great river of ice that was busily carving Hurricane Canyon into shape. There is good evidence that this glacier, never very large, was one of the most persistent in the Wallowas, lasting far longer than the great valley glaciers, possibly even surviving, in stunted form, into recent historic times. Even now, deep in the cirque, great snowfields linger all summer behind the ancient moraines; walking them, you get the eerie feeling that they may decide at any moment to start grinding away downhill, opening crevasses beneath your unwary feet.

The point we sat on was directly opposite this cirque and slightly above its lower lip, although *lip* is perhaps a misleading term because an active little stream has eroded most of it away, cutting a great ragged V into the mountain clear down to Hurricane Creek. The cirque is a thousand feet deep and more than a third of a mile from rim to rim. But again, this description is misleading, for there is really only one rim, one great, continuous, contorted ridge sweeping from the valley floor, around the headwall, and back to the valley in one unanimous, dynamic, almost fluid motion. If it were possible—which it isn't—to walk this ridge from timberline up one arm, across the summit, and back down the other arm to timberline again, the distance covered would be more than three miles. Or, if you started and ended on the valley floor instead of timberline, closer to six.

Just now, though, we weren't interested in matters of scale or of genesis, or in hypothetical journeys around the rims of cirques. We were route-finding. What defenses did the mountain throw up around its summit? What was the best way to breach them? "Best" did not necessarily mean "easiest." We were picky. We wanted a route challenging enough to be interesting but not challenging enough to keep us from the top. We wanted the top, but we wanted a little fun on the way, too.

There appeared to be three general ways to proceed. The simplest way would be to avoid the cirque altogether, walking several miles further up-canyon and then striking left, directly up the south side of the mountain, to the ridge connecting it with the Matterhorn. There would be no cliffs on this route, only a long, sweeping snow climb of four thousand feet. We abandoned it. We did not *want* a long, sweeping snow climb of four thousand feet.

A second possible approach would take us up the outlet stream and into the cirque, right to the base of the headwall, and then diagonally to the left up a steep snow slope that apparently reached all the way to the summit ridge. This would be considerably more varied than the first route, and it would take us close to some pretty hairy-looking cliffs, but it wouldn't take us onto them. There was no more real challenge than the first route. We abandoned this way, too.

That left the way we had picked from the map, the north rim of the cirque, or what we referred to as the "North Ridge." We looked at it carefully and with mounting excitement. Yes, it would surely "go." Timbered slopes up from the valley formed a steep but passable route to the crest. Once on that crest we would be walking a backbone of stone between two abysses, the cirque to our right, the canyon of Thorpe Creek yawning to our left beneath the Thorpe Creek Wall. There would be a few little problems in the way of *gendarmes* and minor cliff bands, but only one of these looked serious. Just at nine thousand feet the ridge was interrupted by a great triangular wall of gray stone, plumb as the side of a house and at least a hundred feet high. We would have to find a way around or over it. And that would give us the challenge we sought.

It was decided, then. The route had been picked, its difficulties explored as thoroughly as possible from a distance. The reconnaissance was over. It was time to go down.

First, though, we would go on up a little ways. Only a couple of hundred feet of easy slopes separated us from the summit of this unnamed Hurricane Divide outrider we had been scrambling up all morning. Might as well go all the way. We moved skyward over wind-packed snow and broken, shaley stone that chimed under our boots like bells. A light wind blew up from the distant world. The peak approached. We were there.

Well, whatever else happened, we had made *one* summit this trip. We stayed awhile, looking at the canyon; and at the snowy line of peaks, a half mile away and a thousand feet above us, that formed the main body of the Hurricane Divide; and at the big, arched, multicolored and immaculate world. Then we went down.

It was nearly dusk when we got back to camp. Since this day's trip had been planned as a short one, we had not taken a lunch, and consequently I had eaten no food, save the morning's breakfast, for nearly two days. It had been even longer since I had really slept. Yet I did not particularly miss either food or sleep. Had someone offered me a meal or a bed I would have accepted it gladly, but I did not crave either one. I felt alert and whole and integrated into my surroundings. I was learning to expect this feeling of wholeness and integration, to accept it as one of the gifts the mountains give to those who venture among them. It was wholeness that had been missing on Pete's Point, wholeness that I had felt after the Backwards Mountain, wholeness and integration that had coursed thrillingly through me as I stood in a dark meadow listening to the cry of a panther. I did not yet fully understand this feeling, or why it occurred, but I was glad it was there.

I helped prepare supper.

I crawled into my sleeping bag.

I thought of the long day, the tooth, the panther, and the cliffs, and the adventures that awaited us on Sacajawea; and finally,
I slept.

V

Our first day on Sacajawea passed in a deceptively leisurely manner.

We began by crawling out of our sleeping bags, late, into the warm sunshine. We ate an unhurried breakfast and lazily broke camp. There was no need to rush; we already knew we weren't going all the way to the summit today. That had been decided yesterday, high on the wall of Hurricane Canyon. We'd never make it in a one-day assault—the mountain was just too damn big. We would go as high as we could today, camp someplace on the North Ridge, and finish the job in the morning. The time lost could be made up by crossing off the layover day after the Matterhorn; with luck, we would still make all four summits.

Laden by the packs, we moved downslope from our vacated campsite, crossed Hurricane Creek on a snowbridge, and attacked the far side. I felt a little thrill of anticipation. We were on the mountain, and climbing, at last! This was to be my first major, expedition-type climb, my first ascent requiring a high camp. At that very moment, halfway around the world, the American Mount Everest expedition—the one that would put Jim Whittaker on the summit of the world—was making its first tentative probes beyond Base Camp on the Khombu Glacier. We would be their distant kin. We were leaving Base Camp and moving upward, through snow, to Camp II. The comparison was obvious and flattering. We stuck to it. In my slide tray today, that is how the pictures are labeled: *Base Camp; Camp II; Camp III.*

There was only one ticklish spot that first day, and it came right at the beginning. The lowest thirty feet or so of the mountain's flank, directly above Hurricane Creek, were steep snow crowned by three feet of vertical rock. A Sunday stroll, except for two things. Our big packs were throwing us off balance; and at the base of the snow, waiting eagerly to make the least little misstep a fatal one, the swollen waters of the creek plunged thundering into the rocky Inner Gorge. Waterfall mists rose from its unseen and churning depths. Swaying under the packs, we moved cautiously up a diagonal line of kicked steps. At the small rock band, each of us paused, placed his axe out of the way, and swung up over the edge. We breathed again. Above, the going was easier; soon we were under trees, on soft, uncompacted snow two to three feet deep. Weighted by the packs, we sank to below our knees. For the first time in the trip we put on snowshoes.

The next few hours were the kind the old hymn refers to as "tedious and tasteless." We wound back and forth through the trees, awkward on our snowshoes, continually searching for the easiest path upward. Occasionally views would open to the west and south, but more often our world was small and closed: slanted white snow, dark tree trunks, and overhead a small patch of blue. It was cold in the shade but pleasant where the sun reached us. Several hours along we paused for lunch in a steep little clearing. Bob and Cliff broke out the food as soon as they got into the sun; I struggled on to the upper line of trees, hoping for a view, and was disappointed. I was getting tired of the damn trees. On Everest, they were already far above timberline. When was our turn going to come?

Above our lunch spot we struggled on for another hour and a half. Then—finally!—the slope began to modulate from steepness into gentleness. Sky blue crept down the spaces between the tree trunks. We had reached the ridge. A few hundred feet beyond was timberline.

In the last grove of trees, tucked into a protected saddle at the base of a prominent little knob, we pitched camp. I was a little disappointed in the choice of location. It was only three in the afternoon. Why not press on for a couple of hours up the ridge? Surely, the closer we got to the summit today the better chance we would have of making it all the way tomorrow! That buttress looked as though it would be difficult and time consuming to surmount. Why not give ourselves as much of a chance as possible? I argued forcibly, but I was overruled. Cliff was tired; Bob wanted a camp with a fire, and we could get no wood further up the mountain. We stayed where we were.

Still, when I got over my disappointment at not continuing, I had to admit that Bob and Cliff had picked a splendid spot for a camp. Beyond our grove the snowy saddle dropped slightly, then swept upward into a broad white triangular slope forty or fifty feet high with a small gray fist of rock at its apex. To the west, snow edged in a clean curve ending in timbered slopes; beyond the space of Hurricane Canyon lay the distant, ragged peaks of the Hurricane Divide. To the east was another space, the thousand-foot-deep gulf of Thorpe Creek Canyon, its sides too steep for trees, the bowl at its head, two miles distant, as cleanly laid out as if it had been drawn by a draftsman. Snow on those Thorpe Creek walls lay at impossibly dizzy angles; cornices overhung them. The ridge humped steeply down to the north, cleaving the two spaces, its backbone studded with gnarled and ancient trees. Suspended in space, we rode the tail of a white dragon. The world was huge.

The knob to the south blocked our view of the mountain. Leaving the packs, Cliff and I scrambled up. As we gained the crest Sacajawea reared up from behind it, white and awesome, her summit still a mile and a half distant and two thousand feet above us. The ridge humped toward it and then thrust suddenly upward, broken by the great triangular face of the buttress. Blue shadow lay on the half-mile-high East Wall, accenting the starkness of its bare rock and hanging, precipitous snowfields. A breeze came from it, distant and Himalayan and cold. *Tomorrow,* we thought, *tomorrow we will stand at the source of that breeze.*

We glissaded back into camp to await the coming night.

Night, at that height, did not fall. Night rose; it rose out of Thorpe Creek, out of the Hurricane, black shadows creeping stealthily to our feet up the cold slopes. For a long moment after dark had swallowed the canyons we rode a swath of pink-tinged snow between two dark and silent seas. Then, slowly, the pink faded. Overhead, the stars were twinkling into being.

On the very lip of the thousand-foot drop into Thorpe Creek,

Bob built his fire. For a little while the fire beat back the night; then the embers cooled, and one by one, the darkness snuffed them out. We crawled back into the tents, to solid and invigorating sleep.

The next day dawned cold and clear, perfect climbing weather. We broke camp early, and slinging on the packs once more, we started up the ridge. To our left Thorpe Creek yawned full of blue shadow, but when we topped the knob south of camp we saw that the East Wall was bathed with rosy light. The only sounds were the creak of the packs and the crunch of climbing boots on crusted snow. The air tasted of morning.

The first of the day's adventures came almost at once. Fifteen minutes from camp, contouring the south side of a tall hump, we came quite suddenly to a small sandy place, snow free, amid talus and wiry krummholz. Tufts of white hair were pressed into the sand, and there was the rounded imprint of a heavy body. I touched the spot; it was still warm. We had roused a mountain goat from his bed, and somewhere nearby, out of sight, he must be watching us. Like the panther tracks in the canyon, this sign of another mammalian presence was oddly comforting. However foolish and quixotic our quest for high and cold places might seem to those who stayed behind, vegetating in the warm dullness of their homes, it was a quest we shared with other living things. The goat was a companion and a fellow adventurer. We moved upward into a suddenly friendlier world.

For the next hour or so the ridge was easy; then the going began to be more difficult. There were gendarmes to bypass, knobs to climb over. Once we came to the edge of a precipice above a saddle and had to backtrack to find a way around. And always there was the enigmatic buttress, drawing ever closer, looming over us, till at last we topped the final knob, bypassed the last gendarme, and came out into the bare and windswept saddle directly beneath that great gray wall. It was just noon.

Over a lunch of cheese and flatbread, washed down with snow-melt, we discussed alternative routes. For some time now, it had been apparent that a bypass to the west would be the best way; but now that we could see that way close up, it didn't look very promising either. Snowfield upon rock upon snowfield, it hung at a dizzying angle above a sheer drop into the great open maw of the big cirque. Rocks beneath that drop-off stuck up through the snow like teeth. Two hundred yards out into the nearest snowfield, a cleaver of scree offered a possible path. But we would have to cross the snow to get to it. And Bob had first handled an ice axe only three days before.

There was another problem, too. While we had been working our way up the last stretches of the ridge, while we had been eating lunch, our perfect day had deserted us. The sky was leaden now, and a wind was rising. It was blizzard weather. We would have to move quickly if we were to complete the climb before the storm hit.

Leaving our packs leaned up against the buttress, we began cutting steps horizontally across the snowfield toward the scree cleaver. The snow was treacherous, four inches of powder over a crusty base, steep enough so that an outstretched hand would touch it if you stood straight. Mist swirled below us in the cirque. It took nearly an hour to make those two hundred yards.

We went back for the packs, ferried them across to the cleaver. In the middle of the steepest section I stepped too near the edge of a step and felt it give way beneath me. The mountain reeled; I threw myself across my ice axe. It went in and held. I had slid three feet. It felt like thirty.

Now the cleaver itself confronted us, six hundred feet of ice-covered gravel nearly as steep as the snowfield. We started up, Cliff in the lead. It was slow work. The glass-slick ice would not hold a boot, and only by clawing at the slope with our axes and taking advantage of every irregularity in the surface could we stay on the mountain at all. We did not rope up; there were no belay stances available. Each of us moved alone. The wind blew, and snow was in it. Several times I slipped, and twice I slid several feet; but each time I was able to regain purchase and go on.

Finally the scree ended in a small patch of snow. There were footprints across the snow, and on the far side Cliff sat on a boulder, beneath an easy rise to the ridge. When Bob joined us a few minutes later, we were able to grin. The buttress was below us!

It was three-thirty in the afternoon. We had been on the cleaver for two hours.

There was no time to lose; we were still a long way from the summit. Quickly, we moved up to the ridge. When we reached the crest, the wind met us with a blast that almost knocked us into Thorpe Creek Canyon, and the air was suddenly filled with swirling snow. We gained the north peak and started along the connecting ridge toward the true summit, walking single file about eight feet below the crest. The air was quieter here, and we could see; but we could hear the wind above, howling across the rock and ice of the mountain's backbone, howling like a gigantic and angry animal. There was great urgency in that sound. This was no place for a bivouac, no place to ride out a storm! We would have to reach the summit, cross it, descend to the saddle of the Matterhorn. And hope to find shelter there before this storm struck us in earnest.

I was in the lead now, setting as rapid a pace as possible over the uneven ground. A curious mixture of feelings was welling up within me: pride and humility, excitement and anxiety and confidence. Pride that we had got so far, under such adverse conditions—but humility, small and quiet, before the overwhelming size and power of the mountain and the storm. Excitement and anxiety about the challenges yet to be overcome—but calm confidence in the outcome. We would survive the storm—I had no doubt about that. And we would almost certainly make the summit. I could see it now, barely a hundred yards away, looming hugely through the thickening snow. In just a few more minutes! . . .

And then a gust of wind hit, and I heard a loud cry from behind me—a cry of mingled horror and disgust. I whirled around.

Bob and Cliff were still on the mountain, still apparently unhurt. But the top of Cliff's pack flapped empty. Far down the rapidly steepening slope into the western cirque whirled a small black object—Cliff's sleeping bag.

We watched while it bounded across several small drops, sped down a hanging snowfield, and disappeared over the lip of a large cliff. For long, heart-stopping moments we didn't see it; then it came into sight again, very tiny, a black speck moving across the vast snowfields of the cirque floor. A thousand feet below us, out in the middle of that white expanse, it finally stopped moving.

Fingers of mist swam about the far wall of the cirque. Small flakes of snow drove at us horizontally.

Cliff checked the straps on my pack and on Bob's to make sure they were tight, so that no more sleeping bags would take off on unscheduled flights. Then we held a conference. The situation was unquestionably serious, perhaps the most serious that any of us had ever faced. We were at nearly ten thousand feet, on an exposed, icy ridge, in the near edge of an approaching blizzard. It was past four, and night was coming in. There were three of us. There were only two sleeping bags.

What to do?

For a short time we toyed seriously with the idea of simply writing off the lost sleeping bag, of continuing on course as planned, over the summit and into a sheltered spot on the far side. There we could erect just one of our two-man tents and squeeze the three of us inside. By placing Cliff between Bob and me, we could probably give him enough heat to stay alive. Or perhaps—Bob had a mummy bag, but mine was envelope-cut, rectangular instead of body-hugging, and maybe Cliff and I could both squeeze inside it.

Probably. Perhaps. Maybe.

Not sure enough. Abandon it.

Then what about retreat? Back the way we had come, back past the buttress, back down the ridge, back to our camp of the night before? There we could find wood and build a fire. And that would surely keep Cliff warm through the night.

No, that wouldn't work either. It had taken us all day to get to where we were. Would it not take us all this stormy night to return? Even assuming we *could* return past that fierce buttress?

We abandoned that possibility too.

And that left us with just one course, just one real hope of success at keeping us all alive into the next day. We would have to abandon the ridge entirely, find a way down into the cirque, and try to recover Cliff's sleeping bag. We would have to do it before nightfall set in. And if that meant forgoing any chance at the summit, well, Cliff was certainly more important than the summit. That was the way it would have to be.

We studied the cirque wall. It dropped off awesomely, black where it was vertical, white everywhere else, obscured now and again by blowing snow. Directly beneath us it was mostly black. We would not go the way the sleeping bag had gone. Think, then. What had that wall looked like from the far side of the canyon?

Snowfields had filled the bottom of the cirque, and then they had swung up and to the left. . . .

And suddenly I saw a way that we might have both the summit *and* the sleeping bag.

Excitedly, I spelled out my plan to the other two. Those cirque snowfields headed out right at the base of the summit block. We could go that far, drop the packs, rush the summit, and then return to pick up our gear and drop down into the cirque to hunt for the bag. The extra run shouldn't take more than ten minutes. Certainly we could spare that much!

Cliff and Bob agreed. We pressed forward into the storm in what was very nearly a dead run. The summit ridge leveled off, dropped down slightly. . . .

And then rose up again. Jutted up, thrust up. Ended all hope for the summit.

We stood at the edge of a boulder slope ten feet high above a small col. The boulders were outlined with new snow. The far side of the col rose grimly into the mist, black and forboding, the summit a vague shape behind it. Only on the east side was it less than vertical. There a steep snowfield hung over what precipices we could not tell. The lines of the face faded and vanished thirty feet below the ridge. Thorpe Creek Canyon was a white, churning nothing.

Sacajawea had set up a spectacular final defense.

I dropped my pack anyway, and with the wind ballooning my parka and tearing the air away from my mouth and nose, I climbed desperately down into the col over the slippery boulders. Perhaps, I thought, thing were not as bad as they looked. But close up, I could see that they were. In our condition, and in this weather, it would take us more than an hour to mount that step. We had given ourselves ten minutes and had been reluctant about doing even that.

We would have to give up.

I snapped a picture. I urinated off the Thorpe Creek Wall. The wind caught my stream and flung it into nothing, into the wall of screaming snow.

We started down.

The conquest of a mountain brings a sense of fulfillment, a sense of peace, a sense of unity with the big world beneath the climber's feet. By contrast, failure—especially failure as high as we had failed—brings only frustration. And it was frustration we felt now, frustration settling over us like a thick blanket as, deep in the cirque, on a protected little knoll at the top edge of the timber, we pitched camp. We had failed. Cliff's sleeping bag had been recovered, miraculously undamaged. Nobody would sleep cold that night. But we had failed.

Glumly, with no great ardor, around a fire that gave no heat, we considered the remainder of our shattered trip. Sawtooth and Twin were now definitely out. But we were still high on Sacajaweja. Perhaps we could wait out the storm, and the avalanche danger after the storm, and salvage a summit yet. Perhaps. But the idea generated little enthusiasm. Snow was falling in thick white flakes, obscuring the dark crags thousands of feet above, obscuring the night. The mountain's black arms enfolded us. She had beaten us back, but now she would rock us to sleep. One by one we left the fire, left the stagnant and dying conversation, burrowed into the tents. Sleep came, heavy and dreamless and deep.

Snow was still falling the next morning. The world had shrunk to a ball of cotton, fifty feet in diameter, blurred and quiet and cold. We moved aimlessly about the camp like trapped animals. Cliff started a snow cave: If we're going to wait it out, he said, we might as well be comfortable. Bob and I didn't help him. The wait was appealing less and less. Summit be damned. We had made a try; it was a heroic try; it had failed; why try, and fail, again? Cliff railed at us, but he railed in vain. The trip was over.

By eleven o'clock we were on our way out.

We threw the packs together hastily, leaving most of the remaining food. Think of it as an offering: The animals would eat it. We put the packs on. Equipment bulged in odd places, but no matter, we would not be unpacking again until in the safety of our homes. We strapped on snowshoes. We started.

The descent was unmemorable. There were no colors, only black and white. We crossed the broad white cirque floor toward a black funnel of trees and moved in among them, following the twisting white path of the snow-covered outlet stream. The stream descended the mountain at a high angle. So did we. We slid, we stumbled, we crawled. More than once we fell through the snow into the gurgling water. New snow kept falling.

Somehow we got across Hurricane Creek, but I don't remember how. I do remember struggling up the far side, finding the trail in the middle of a snow-covered meadow, fleeing along it toward the car. I remember slipping, falling across my ice axe, the adze gashing my parka, gashing my shirt and sweater, leaving a painful mark on my forearm that would take years to fully heal. I remember getting up and going on. Down at the lower elevations the snow had turned to a cold, hard, and desolate rain. The clouds had closed in and followed us, blotting out the mountains. There was nothing here, nothing for us, nothing that human beings could possibly want. Nothing but snow and rain and cold. We ran.

Finally the car appeared, small and welcoming under the dripping trees. We tossed our packs in and climbed in after them. It was dank and cold inside, but the heater would soon fix that. Bob turned the key; the motor growled smoothly into life, a typical Volkswagen air-cooled rattle. It was, under the circumstances, the most beautiful sound in the world. The trip had been over, in spirit, from the time we had begun the glissade into the cirque to search for Cliff's sleeping bag. Now it was over in reality.

We fled down the road, away from the mountains, back toward the distant, welcoming town.

VI

It took me a while to get over Sacajawea.

For several months I planned no climbs, took part in no climbs, did not seek the company of other climbers. Cliff proposed an ascent of Mt. Rainier to cap our junior year; I went along with the plan for a while, then backed out a week before finals. Word from Bob Lawrence that he would not be returning to the Northwest that summer failed to shake my composure. It no longer seemed important. Paradoxically, now that I could begin to qualify as an experienced climber, the urge to climb was deserting me. Sacajawea had stolen it. I read of the English composer Ralph Vaughan Williams, lamenting in his old age: "I have struggled all my life to conquer amateurish technique, and now that I have mastered it, it seems too late to make any use of it." The words hit home. I had conquered mountaineering technique, but I no longer cared. I had the strength to make use of it, and the youth, but I could not muster the enthusiasm.

I still went to the mountains. I still hiked among them and enjoyed them. My backpack did not gather dust. The difference was that for the moment, at any rate, I no longer sought summits. And this seemed strange, because not so long ago—Eagle Cap was less than two years in the past—the summit, and the struggle to reach it, had been my single, unified reason for going into the mountains at all. Then, the trail had been something to endure before climbing;

now, the trail was beginning to be something to be enjoyed for itself. Why? I don't know, but I have a hunch that Sacajawea had a great deal to do with it. I was adventured out. After five days of toothaches, panthers, blizzards, lost sleeping bags, buttresses, traps at the top of snowfields, and impassable final summit steps, I had been through all the adventure I needed for a while. I was ready to stop beating the peaks over the head and start listening to them instead. And maybe I would hear the answers to my Pete's Point questions.

In April, less than a month after Sacajawea, the Outing Club held an overnight to a place called Seven-Mile Camp, in Eagle Creek Canyon, just east of Bonneville Dam in the Columbia River Gorge. I went along. The trail was pasted to the middle of a basalt wall, halfway between creek and tiny sliver of sky. Waterfalls laced the wall; the trail went around them, above them, beside them, behind them. Eagle Creek Canyon was filled with a fine spray. Moss and ferns clung to the basalt wall, grew upon it, covered it. The thunder of falling water was constant. In the morning, after the night at Seven-Mile, a small group detached itself from the main body to explore further up the trail before turning about to trudge, over the same ground, back to the cars. Six months before, at Aneroid Lake, I had led such a sortie; now I did not even go along. I had no desire to rush headlong through new country. I would spend the time, instead, becoming more familiar with country already covered. Melody—the girl from Aneroid Lake, from the trip home in Conrad White's car—would come with me. We meandered back toward the trailhead. When we were still a mile out, the group that had explored further passed us, going full tilt; they had reached a point several miles beyond camp, turned around, regained the overnight spot, picked up their packs, and pressed on without stopping; they would beat us to the cars by a full twenty minutes. I felt a twinge of pity. What in the world were they *seeing* at that pace?

May passed, and June. I did not climb Rainier with Cliff. I went home instead, back to work for Washington State University, this time as number-two man on the campus garbage truck.

July came, dry and heavy and hot. With my parents and my younger brothers and sisters, I tried the Eagle Creek approach on the Wallowas. We drove down for the day and we ambled, rather than hiked, the Aneroid Lake trail as far as Four-Mile Bridge. On twice-familiar ground, equipped with a new camera and with certain knowledge that no climb would take place this trip, I sought diligently to block out the mountains and concentrate on the flowers; tried to *feel* the country, to get in tune with it, rather than to conquer it. It didn't work. These mountains were still too much the Wallowas of my preclimbing youth. I tried hard to only want to go as far as our ramble might take us, but when we turned around I could not stifle my disappointment at not going further. Flowers were no substitute for summits—not in the Wallowas, not yet. The mountains were oppressive, almost as oppressive as they had been during the blizzard that had aborted the summit thrust on Sacajawea. Moodily, I followed my family home. I would not return, not that year, not for flowers.

August: summer's end. Cliff, who was transferring to Columbia University in New York, invited me to join him for a farewell-to-the-Northwest backpacking trip through the Olympics. I accepted. His parents dropped us, late one afternoon, near the end of the Dungeness River Road. In two and a half days we advanced twenty miles to Royal Basin. It rained. We camped under an overhanging rock. For three days we stayed under that rock, like beetles, emerging in rare intervals of sun to scale the walls of the basin and look for a way over the hill to Deception Creek. One pass was steep and shaley; a second led to a slope too steep to negotiate with the packs; a third didn't even lead to Deception Creek. I put a foot through a snowbridge on the Surprise Glacier, dropping up to my hip into a crevasse sixty feet deep. Fortunately, the other foot remained on solid ice. Fog closed in, and more rain. Cliff wanted to try the shaley pass. I refused. I wanted to go home. Cliff, quite properly, was disgusted. As he had done on Sacajaweja, he railed. I didn't budge. Silently, resignedly, Cliff put on his pack and led the way back toward the Dungeness River Road. Eight hours later we were phoning his parents from a roadside grocery, having covered twenty-five miles, with full packs, in that one short day. It was an accomplishment that made up, at least in a small way, for our failure to get to Deception Creek. Cliff decided to speak to me again. We parted on good terms. He flew east to Columbia; I went back to Whitman.

Then, for seven months, almost nothing. . . .

VII

I peered out of the tent door. Big flakes of snow wheeled gently through the shadowless gray air. Beyond them, beyond the silent and indistinct conifers, the black walls of Hurricane Canyon, invisible but overpoweringly present, heaved upward into the cotton sky. Closer than that, closer than the trees, closer than all but the nearest snowflakes, Bob Zimmerman knelt in the snow and coaxed a tiny fire into life.

It was like waking up in the middle of a television rerun.

I shook my head to clear it. Let's see: We left Walla Walla yesterday. Saturday. That's right. So today must be Sunday, and we should be at Slick Rock Creek. That's odd. I don't remember trees at Slick Rock Creek. Cliff—

Another figure materialized out of the snowflakes. Not Cliff. Too tall and slender, head shape wrong. . . . Got it! Cliff's in New York, Larry's here instead, it's 1964 instead of 1963, and this is Sacajawea attempt number 2. Bob and I have been dumb enough to try it *again.*

I pulled myself out of the tent and went to join the others, sinking to my knees in loose, powdery white stuff with each step. It seemed strange how snow conditions could vary from year to year. According to the calendar we were two weeks later in the season this spring, but going by the snow we were at least a month earlier. The last two miles of the Hurricane Canyon road were buried and impassable; we had been forced to cover them on snowshoes. The

parking lot where we had left the car last year had three feet of
snow in it. More snow was falling as we walked. We hadn't made
Slick Rock Creek; we were camped less than a hundred yards beyond the road's end, within spitting distance of the wilderness
boundary, in the grove of trees split by the trail just before it
leaps outward onto the steep, exposed section above the river that
had given us so much trouble last year. We had reached that spot
shortly after lunch and had stayed for a number of reasons, not the
least of which was that we were too tired to go any further.
Snowshoeing is hard work, and we all had been wintered out of
shape. But it didn't matter. Taking a little extra time on the way in
wouldn't hurt us. We had time. Bob and I had laid our plans much
more carefully and much less grandiosely this year. Our goal was
Sacajawea, period. No four peaks, no day in high camp, no
transferring from side to side of the canyon. We had nine days' food
on our backs and Sacajawea in front of us, and we were prepared
to spend the entire nine days, if necessary, reaching that single
summit. This time, by god, we would make it.

A party of two is insufficient for winter climbing; three is minimal,
for safety reasons. Ideally, Cliff should have flown out from New
York to join us, but of course he couldn't. So we had nabbed a substitute. Larry Chitwood was medium height, blond, skinny, and
possessed of phenomenal amounts of stamina and drive. A math
major turned music major, who would eventually and unexpectedly wind up as a Forest Service geologist, Larry was probably my
best friend at Whitman. But despite our friendship and our mutual
interest in the mountains, we had never climbed or hiked together
before this. Sacajawea would be the first time.

It would be the first time, that is, provided it got off the ground.
Just now that was looking questionable. It was still snowing, big
heavy vision-blocking flakes accumulating at the rate of about an
inch an hour. It did not appear to be thinking of letting up soon.
Just ahead, Bob and I knew, was that tricky spot above the river.
We had no desire to tackle it in *this* stuff. We were a hundred yards
from the road, we were less than that from the wilderness boundary, and we were stopped.

Still, it wasn't as discouraging as it might have been. Close as we
might be to the road, that road was not operable; it was two full

miles, by snowshoe, to the car. So we were definitely wilderness-isolated. Since Sacajawea was our only goal this year, we had a number of spare days in the schedule, and we could afford to play things cautiously, to wait out the storm, to wait out several storms if need be. It was not really cold, not for the mountains—the temperature in our little grove was hanging somewhere around thirty degrees Fahrenheit. And our surroundings were beautiful, almost criminally so. Freed from the hurry-up, break-camp-and-trudge-and-set-up-again that had been the norm for all climbing trips I had yet been on, we could enjoy that beauty. We watched snow crystals build into delicate, interlocking patterns on the tents, on the tent ropes, on the filigreed branches of the trees. We fed the slender, dancing flame of our fire, listened to the satisfying crackle of its eating, watched as it melted its way down through the snow to a circle of soft brown earth that gradually grew outward beyond the immediate circle of burning. Putting on snowshoes, we sought downed and dry wood among the silent, snow-covered forms of the trees. Sounds were echoless, muffled, reverberation free. From the cotton-soft thunder of Hurricane Creek, leaping whitely among white stones, we drew more than water; we drew also the sight of a small gray body, winged, darting among rapids. Water ouzel. Like the panther and the mountain goat of last year, a friend. We were not alone. There were no other humans about, but this was unimportant. Perhaps, considering where we were, we were closer kin to these animals than to other humans, anyway.

Slowly, serenely, detailed in white, the day passed. Gently and continuously, quiet snowflakes stroked the approaching night.

Sometime during that night the snow stopped. We awoke to grayness, but it was a grayness punctuated by small and swiftly moving patches of sun. Overhead, at intervals, the clouds made blue windows. The weather was changing. We broke camp and moved south, up-canyon, awkward on our snowshoes under the heavy packs. We moved through a dream of snow. Snow burdened the trees, snow hung on the cliffs, snow cushioned the trail and lay in a white, unconsolidated blanket across the meadows. New snow, soft and untrammeled. We could almost see the spaces between the crystals.

The day was not without its excitement. Each broad meadow was a blank and a challenge, trail and nontrail buried impartially beneath the sameness of snow. In the center of each clearing we would stand, slowly scanning the far side, looking for a break in the wall of trees that would indicate the further course of the trail. Sometimes we found it on the first try; more often we would have to back up and look again, a second time, perhaps a third time. Clouds shifted in the heights of the canyon, alternately exposing and covering snow-burdened spires of rock. High on the walls, precarious whiteness threatened avalanches. It was not an empty threat. The upper canyon was crisscrossed by fresh avalanche tracks. We ate lunch on the tail of one. Another very nearly started beneath Bob as he traversed less than six feet from the lip of the narrow, waterfall-filled Inner Gorge; only his ice axe and practically instantaneous reflexes kept him from going over the edge along with the snow that moments before had been beneath his right snowshoe. Shortly beyond this near-disaster was Slick Rock Creek. Here lay the track of the largest avalanche we had seen yet; the ledge we had pitched our tents on last year lay squarely in its path and was buried under tons of fresh debris. "Holy cow," said Bob, with feeling. We sought safety beyond Slick Rock, in a grove of trees that appeared to be big and old, and therefore not in a likely avalanche path. The ground beneath the grove was steep but buried beneath more than four feet of snow; carving ledges for the tents was easy. Hurricane Creek foamed by beneath snowbridges less than twenty feet away. Immediately beyond the creek, a blank and snow-swept canyon wall—the bottom flank of Sacajawea—leaped skyward. It was a spectacular and terrifying spot.

Quickly, we settled into the new camp. But the day was not done with us yet. Dusk was almost upon us; but it only takes an instant to undo a trip, and that instant was about to arrive.

It began simply enough. Larry had been dissatisfied with the manner in which we were forced to follow the fire down through the snow at our wilderness-boundary camp. Why not dig the pit *first*, here, and build the fire on solid ground? Bob and I agreed. We laid out a circle large enough to encompass the three of us plus fire and began removing snow from the center of it. The upper layers were easily scooped out with our gloved hands, but further down we got into the consolidated, icelike base, and that was not so easy. We worked it with our ice axes, breaking it up with short, rapid strokes of the adze, digging the loose material out by hand, then taking up the axes again. This process was still too slow for Larry. Motioning us aside, he went at the stuff with the pick end of his axe head, swinging the handle in great wicked strokes. On the third or fourth stroke he miscalculated. The pick swung down, grazed the snow, deflected, and buried itself an inch deep in his right leg, just below the kneecap.

Bob applied a three-inch-square gauze pad, held on by adhesive tape. It soaked through and was discarded. A second pad also soaked through. Someone—Larry or Bob—rigged a butterfly bandage. That stopped the bleeding, but the least little motion of Larry's leg would pop it off. Though he was not making a scene of it, he was in severe pain. We helped him to one of the tents, where he lay consciously *not* flexing his leg. Bob and I went back to moving snow. Hanging over us were numerous questions. Would Larry's knee infect? Would he be able to use the leg, to climb? Or would we have to carry him out? It appeared likely that it would be some time before we knew the answers. We would have to amend our schedule with another layover day. At least one.

We finished the fire pit. It was an architectural marvel, considering the circumstances—four feet deep on the uphill side, two on the downhill; a little snow-floored, roofless room with built-in benches lined with pine boughs on either side of a dirt-hearthed fireplace made all of snow and complete with chimney. The chimney drew; smoke bellowed from it when we lit the fire. Larry hobbled over from his tent to help prepare supper. We discussed the future of the trip but came to no conclusion. *Tomorrow, tomorrow we'll see.*

It was a colder night than the previous ones had been. I woke up shivering several times; each time, I curled myself into a tighter ball and went back to sleep. Lying beside me, unable to bend his injured leg, Larry was not faring so well. Morning light, cold and gray and cheerless, invaded the tent. I awoke ready for the day and glanced at Larry. He lay on his back, staring glumly at the ceiling of the tent from the folds of his sleeping bag. "Sleep well?" I asked. He grinned sardonically: "Are you kidding?" Only his face moved. "I didn't sleep a wink! If I stuck my head out of the bag I was afraid I'd freeze to death and if I kept it inside I was afraid I'd smother to death! I was awake all night! It was the only way I could stay alive!" Light grew in the tent, then exploded as the sun leaped over the canyon rim. We crawled out into a sparkling world. It would have been a perfect day to move on up the mountain. But Larry's knee was a question mark that had not yet been resolved. We would have to stay where we were.

The morning was sunny, windless, and comparatively warm. Bob sprawled shirtless on an orange poncho, soaking up sun, while Larry and I explored the immediate vicinity of the camp. We did not get far. Larry's leg functioned properly and with a minimum of pain, but a normal walking motion would draw the wound open and renew bleeding in it. We could not get a bandage to hold against this tendency. The future of the trip remained in doubt.

Afternoon. Bob and I went off on a reconnaissance trip, leaving Larry behind with strict orders to stay off his leg and give it a chance to heal. As we had done the year before, we moved up the west wall of the canyon for a view across to Sacajawea. This time, though, we climbed to the south instead of to the north of Slick Rock Creek. The going was much easier. Soon we were high on the wall, with the mountain blossoming into view. It looked snowy and avalanche fraught and extraordinarily high. Bob shook his head: "I wonder." We moved back to camp. Larry had not been following orders. He met us with a smile: "I finally rigged a bandage that stays put!" He had spent the whole time we were gone perfecting that bandage. His technique: Put it on, run full tilt up the side of the canyon opposite camp, come back down, see if it's still there. Eventually he had devised one that was. So there was new hope. We went, all three of us this time, to explore the lower part of the route to the North Ridge of Sacajawea. It had not changed a great deal from last year. Powdery snow lay under trees at a steep angle, and even on our snowshoes we floundered. These were the worst sort of conditions for Larry's knee. It did not open again, but it began to malfunction. Soon he was limping, and less than a quarter of a mile up the mountain, we turned around and headed back to camp.

I remember only one thing from the rest of the afternoon, and

that was the discovery, near dusk, of two large mosquitoes, old beyond their span and near-dormant with the cold, lurching Lazarus-
like through the shadowy snow. They were too cold to bite us; and
besides, any mosquito so determined to live that it could make it
through a winter at that elevation deserved all the respect one could
grant it. We left them alone. *Requiem aeternam dona eis. . . .*

Heat from last night's fire had altered the shape of our chimney
somewhat, but it still functioned. We kindled new flames in the fireplace, and as the dark and the cold closed in, we faced the raw fate
of the expedition squarely for the first time. We had all the data.
Now a decision could be put off no longer; this weather was not
likely to hold, and to wait an extra day would very likely mean that
a new storm would make the decision for us.

We talked and we planned and we thought, and gradually the
many possibilities around us resolved themselves into three worth
exploring further. The most attractive of these, in the context of the
original plan, would be simply to continue on schedule: to spend
tomorrow moving camp to the North Ridge of Sacajawea and to
climb the peak the next day from high camp. We would not make
the mistakes we had made in 1963; we would make camp higher
along the ridge, and we would make the summit thrust without
packs, returning to our ridge camp for a second night. But attractive
as this plan appeared, there were several things wrong with it. It
meant trusting the weather to remain beneficent for *two* more days,
not just one. It meant climbing through the loose snow on the side
of the North Ridge, climbing under the worst possible conditions for
Larry's damaged knee, and doing it with full fifty-pound packs. As
for Larry, who had slept so cold last night, there seemed an added
disadvantage: not one, not two, but a minimum of *three* more
nights in the snow. With two whole legs he would have been game
to try it, but the combination of factors was too much for him. He
would go if *we* went, yes; but he was less than anxious to try it, and
he would not guarantee that he would come back.

But that didn't necessarily mean that we would have to give up
Sacajawea. There was another possibility. Suppose we rushed the
peak from where we were, climbing without packs, doing the whole
thing in one long day? By starting at three in the morning—not an
unusual hour for climbers to set out—we would catch the snow un-

der the trees in its easiest, crustiest condition, and Larry would be likely to have little trouble with it. And it would reduce the number of further nights in the snow from three to two. This plan was attractive enough to consider seriously; but as we took it up and looked it over, we could see problems with it, too. It would be an awfully long day. Bob and I remembered the buttress; suppose it was even harder to pass this year than last? We would risk getting caught by nightfall high on the mountain with all our gear several thousand feet below us. If a storm were to blow up, we would not have the equipment to bivouac and wait it out. And since a camp on the ridge would be somewhat warmer than a camp in the canyon— canyons, at night, tend to be rivers of cold air that the ridges sit above—we would very likely be trading two nights of semicomfort for one night of pure frozen hell.

That put Plan Number One back in the running.

But there was a third possibility, too. It was not an attractive possibility, but we had to consider it. *Perhaps, after all, the accident to Larry's knee had put the mountain once again beyond our reach.*

Perhaps it was simply too big a job for a leg that had just had an ice axe buried in it. Perhaps, for the second straight year, we would have to forget about the summit of Sacajawea.

This did not necessarily mean that the trip was a failure, I pointed out. We could still get a climb in. There were plenty of lesser summits around, peaks that would command not nearly so much of our accident-limited resources. Suppose we were to tackle one of those, instead? There was a good candidate at hand—in fact, you might say we were sitting on it. Just at the head of Slick Rock Creek the Hurricane Divide humped up into a high, snowy, imposing, and as far as we could tell, officially unnamed peak. We had given it a name of our own last year: Deadman Point, after a small body of water, Deadman Lake, cupped in a cirque high on its north side. The topographic map said it was almost 9,600 feet high. I reminded the others of the view we had gotten of it that afternoon from Sacajawea's flank, thrusting up in the west, majestic and white and alone, into the blue sky. Surely here was a peak both within our grasp and worthy of that grasp! Bob nodded slowly. "I wouldn't mind climbing Deadman," he said. Larry hesitated, probably feeling desperately unhappy at the prospect of having the trip plans changed so drastically solely on his account. I hastened to assure him that it wasn't solely on his account. I was not too anxious to spend more than one further night in that cold camp, either. And if we started Deadman early enough—that would be wise, anyway, the snow would be better—we could be back in camp shortly after noon, with a summit under our belts and with plenty of daylight left to pack out to the car. By this time tomorrow we might have brought the trip to a successful conclusion and be home in bed.

And that is how it happened.

We went to our sleeping bags that night sometime between eight-thirty and nine. We were up six hours later. The sky was still pitch-black, and the air was unearthly cold, but neither fact concerned us greatly. Moving would keep us warm. And since our ascent plan called for simply striking out uphill as directly as possible immediately behind the tents, detail vision was unnecessary. We ate a quick cold breakfast and started. The way climbed steeply through heavy timber. Soon we were high above the dark valley. Overhead the black sky paled to gray, then darkened into an intense and saturated blue. The jagged peaks at the south end of the Hurricane Divide turned rose, then yellow, then brilliant white; light flowed down the mountains and cupped in the quiet canyon. The day was upon us.

We reached timberline shortly after eight in the morning. Before us lay literally thousands of acres of snow, dazzling white, accented by rock colors, yellow and brown and black, where there were cliffs angled too steeply for the snow to cling. We climbed a ridge all snow on the south side, all yellow rock on the north. The angle of ascent eased; cornices appeared, heavy and graceful, over the right-hand cliffs. The ridge climbed to eighty-one-hundred feet, dropped to eight thousand again, then swept upward in one final massive thrust to the summit ridge 1,500 feet above. It looked horrendously steep. We tackled it. It *was* horrendously steep. I worried slightly about Larry's knee, but evidently it wasn't bothering him. We climbed upward in a steady, ground-devouring rest-step. The ridge was marked by a thin line of bare, broken rock between snow slopes to the south and cornices to the north. We alternated between rock and snow, uncertain which was less difficult. Midway in the final push, Bob stepped too far to the north. There was a muffled *Yaaaa* . . . as part of a cornice gave way beneath him; he spread his arms and caught them on the edges of the hole his body had made. Larry and I pulled him out, and we all looked into the hole—through the hole—several hundred feet down the cliff face to sunlit, distant snow. We stuck to the rock or south of it after that. The lines of the face and of the ridge converged in a single point. That point came closer. It was there. The angle suddenly eased off; to the north, at the far end of a gentle, snowy, wind-shingled ridge marked by two short steep stretches, we could see the summit. In ten minutes we were on it. It was slightly after ten in the morning.

The sky had lost most of its color; clouds were gathering in a long mass across the southern horizon, and small outriders from that mass, detached and lonely, were drifting over our heads. The change of weather I had feared might catch us on Sacajawea seemed to be taking place. But here it did not matter; we had reached the summit, and we would have plenty of time to descend. We stood in the snow and looked out over the snowy world. To the south and the west, tumbled masses of peaks rolled out to meet the sky, so many and so confused as to largely escape naming, though we could pick out a few: The white pyramid of Cusick Mountain, for instance, and the spire-topped bulge of Needle Point, and the distinctive, sawed-off dome of Eagle Cap. Closer at hand, sweeping up to us from the south and falling away again to the north, the high, white Hurricane Divide flung its summits for miles across the scene. Our peak was one of them. It was like standing on one of the teeth of a giant saw.

The crest of the divide and its sides downward for several thousand feet were bare, bleak rock and snow. Beyond the antarctic-appearing ridge to the north, beyond and six thousand feet down, plains and low hills stretched northward out of sight. Two thousand feet below us to the west lay the iced-over basin of Frances Lake; to the northeast, closer and higher, looking as though it must be solidly frozen right through, lay Deadman Lake. And eastward . . .

Eastward lay Sacajawea.

Beyond the earth-cleaving void of Hurricane Canyon she rose, grew, was piled, crag upon cliff upon snowfield, magnificent, lonely, and huge. A mile to the south of her, connected to her by a high white ridge, the black Matterhorn thrust his summit to a height scarcely seven feet lower than hers. Between them the two peaks dominated the visible world, thrust out of it and above it, massive and commanding and cold. According to the map, I remembered incredulously, the peak we were on was less than three hundred feet lower. It was a fact that simply refused to register. There is a loftiness about a great mountain that has nothing to do with the raw physical measurement called height above sea level. Deadman Point didn't have it. Sacajawea did.

I climbed the peak with my eyes, using the route we had forged last year and had planned to use again. There was the North Ridge, a flying buttress amidst a maze of cliffs. We had camped on that ridge, *there, beneath that pinnacle . . . there we had climbed and scrambled . . . there, there on that awesome white sweep of face, there we had bypassed the buttress.* The buttress was large and gray black. *There Cliff had lost his sleeping bag . . . and there . . .*

There we had turned back.

With an effort, I tore myself back into the present. I was on a summit, a high summit, Deadman Point. I had set a goal and I had reached it. The trip was a success. Why did I continue to gaze across the canyon, to gaze at failure, and to remember it with longing?

And now, shifting my gaze back and forth across the canyon, from the summit of Deadman to the summit of Sacajawea, I began to think that I might perceive the small beginnings of an answer. This answer lay not on the summits themselves but among the barriers before the summits. Sacajawea had many such barriers and we had conquered them all, all but the very last. Deadman had none, so we had conquered none. Sacajawea had been a route-finder's dream, requiring skill, foresight, and the ability to sort through the pieces of the terrain ahead in order to find that chunk of it that would be the most easily surmountable. And Deadman? Well, Deadman had required endurance. That was all.

Still, endurance was something, and success was not to be sneered at. We had overcome injury, adverse weather, and incredibly steep—if uniform—terrain; and we had reached in winter the summit of one of the highest Wallowa peaks. We had proved it could be done. And our good friend Mr. White, of the Outing Club, would have to eat his words.

I picked up my ice axe and motioned to the others. Somehow, more than forty-five minutes had slipped by. If we were going to make the car by nightfall, we would have to begin moving; there was a lot of work ahead of us yet. Bob nodded and started off. Larry followed. I took a last look around, snapped a final picture, and hurried after them, leaving the summit to the winds and sun.

The descent was uneventful and rapid, a series of glissades, the final one bringing us out of the trees, across the trail, between the tents, and almost into the creek. We ate lunch, scattering the remainder of our food around for the animals as we had the year before (no sense carrying it out; we wouldn't need it now). The tents were taken down, rolled up, and tied into place on our packs. The packs were shouldered. Circling toward the trail on our snowshoes, we turned for one last look at the ex-camp. At that moment, like a signal of departure, the heat-weakened chimney fell slowly and soundlessly into the fire pit. We laughed out loud. Five miles ahead was the car. We would reach it before suppertime.

Our feet followed each other—stamp, stamp, stamp—in their snowshoes down the white trail toward home.

VIII

Having now been beaten back twice by Sacajawea, Bob and I temporarily turned our attentions elsewhere.

From the summit of Deadman Point, looking north along the Hurricane Divide, we had seen close at hand an odd, intriguing peak—a dome, gentle and snowy and 9,600 feet high, which bore precisely on its rounded summit a pair of sharp, needlelike rock spires fifty to seventy-five feet tall. Those spires were totally out of keeping with the character of the rest of the mountain, and seeing them there had given us a little shock, rather like finding a nude in a picture of the ladies' auxiliary. The mountain was called Twin Peaks, and it had been a secondary goal of our first Sacajaweja expedition. Now we made it a primary goal.

We tackled it for the first time shortly after school was out. I had nabbed a job as janitor for the Walla Walla First Congregational Church, which put me in town for the summer; Bob, his association with Whitman at an end, was taking a couple of months off before moving to a new job in San Francisco. Part of that time he intended to spend backpacking alone through the Wallowas, and Twin Peaks would be a good warm-up for that. We laid our plans casually. We would drive to a place called Lapover Ranch, some distance up the Lostine Canyon road; leave the car; and pack in three miles to an overnight camp at Frances Lake. Approximately two hours of shale-scrambling the next day would bring us to the base of those incongruous pinnacles on top of Twin, and we would have the rest of the day to figure out how to get to the top of them. It was a plan that seemed easily workable—what could go wrong?—so we didn't pay a great deal of attention to detail, a mistake that (as usual) would prove costly. At the last minute we recruited two extra climbers, Steve Mason and Harmon Grahn, students whom Bob knew through his classes; I was totally unfamiliar with either of them. Neither was an experienced climber. Outfitting them took all morning and part of the afternoon of the day we were supposed to leave, and by the time we rolled out of Walla Walla, in two separate Volkswagens, it was almost two o'clock.

The sky was gray and bilious above the town of Lostine, but the mountains were visible and now and again there was even a tiny patch of blue in one gap or another between the clouds. We were not unduly alarmed. Soon the Lostine Canyon road was under our wheels. It was the first time I had been that way since my earliest Wallowa trip, three years before, and I was amazed and intrigued by the difference those three years had wrought in the way I looked at the scenery. It was a difference that was apparent almost from the beginning, as we threaded the moraine remnants at the canyon mouth and skirted the long alluvial plain behind them. *My God,* I thought with a shock, *there was another Wallowa Lake here once. How could I have missed it? It's plain as the nose on your face.* Though I remembered Bob Lawrence saying something about an "old lake bed" as we drove this section of the road on our way in to Eagle Cap, I had not seen it. To my unpracticed nineteen-year-old eye, the morainal material had been a group of odd hills, the alluvial plain only a flat spot on the valley floor. Now, four summers later, I found myself without difficulty seeing a scene as it must have once been—a long, shallow lake at the foot of a receding glacier. It was like looking beneath the skin of time. I was absolutely delighted with myself. It was a dangerous state in which to begin a climb.

It was slightly past four o'clock when we reached Lapover Ranch. The evening was prematurely dark, and a light rain had begun to mist down; across the canyon a great peak, steep faced and streaked with snow, faded in and out of a relentless cloud veil. Small pieces of the veil, rent from it, lodged and dissolved far down the mountain's flank. Others seemed to be born of the high couloirs, to billow up, detach themselves, and drift off to join the main mass. By rights we should have read those signs for what they were and camped at the cars. But it was "just three miles" to Frances Lake, and even at under a mile an hour we should make it by seven-thirty. It was June: Light should be with us till nine. And the parking lot was dank and dismal and disfigured by the great clanking presence of a gigantic yellow bulldozer. We pulled on rain gear and wriggled into the packs. The drivers locked their cars. We started.

Almost at once we lost the trail. Frances Lake is served by a secondary trail, neither well maintained nor commonly used, and its beginning, that season, was indistinct. We found ourselves in the middle of a steep, brush-covered hillside, following a hopeless maze of indistinct game trails. Damp brush overhung the trails and rubbed against our legs. Soon our pants were soaked through. Finally, years later (though it was probably really only about twenty minutes), we came out quite by accident onto the human trail again, a broad, level section of it stretching across the hillside like an avenue. It was as if Lancelot had discovered the Holy Grail. We started jubilantly along it—the wrong way. Soon we were going downhill. Turn around, then—there must be a switchback back there the way we had come. There was. It overlooked a steep little valley rising to high crags that lost themselves in the rain. Down the center of it, seemingly born directly of the rain itself, a determined little stream foamed and roared in what was essentially one long waterfall. It was a scene better suited to the Olympics than to the Wallowas. I took a picture to show to Cliff. We pressed on. Soon we were high on the lower slopes of something called Marble Point, passing alternately through wet groves of trees and wetter brush slopes. Fog closed in, then lifted to reveal a sweeping, if wet, view up-canyon toward Two Pan Camp and the forks of the Lostine. The valley was a perfect, uniform glacial U, as even as if it had come from the hand of a draftsman. Like the moraine-and-alluvial-plain combination earlier that day, it seemed to jump up and shout at me, and once again I reacted with amazement at how easy it was becoming to read the landscape. On Sacajawea and on Deadman I had looked hard to spot the glacial signs that I knew were there, knew because I had been told. Here I hadn't been told, but they were practically hitting me over the head. That must mean I had finally learned what to look for, and apparently I was doing it without thinking. It was a comforting, confidence-generating sensation, and just about the last satisfying emotion I would get out of this ill-starred trip. The fog closed in again, and we walked on.

There was a spring in a dark grove of trees, then a rock outcrop looking out, in this weather, over nothing. We turned a corner into a short dead-end canyon, reached its headwall, and began ascending a ladder of switchbacks with branches never more than twenty feet long, often much shorter. Sometimes as little as six feet of trail separated one from the next. We moved upward tiredly into gathering and rainy darkness. Snowbanks appeared with increasing frequency, blotting out the trail. Soon it was gone completely. The snow was soft, and our feet sank into it a foot or more with each step. We struggled up the hill. It went on interminably. High on the right, gaunt crags faded into and out of vision. The angle of the snow had not changed. Perhaps it went on forever. Foot by foot we gained altitude. Now we were no longer looking for the trail, or even the top of this endless ridge. We were looking for some-place—anyplace!—where we could pitch two tents. It was already past eight, nearly four hours since we had left the cars. We should have been at the lake by seven-thirty. What was the matter with this goddamned mountain, anyhow?

At eight-thirty, with the slope still stretching infinitely before us, we came to a long horizontal bulge in the snow, not so much a ledge as a ripple, noticeably less steep than the rest but still quite far from level. It would have to do. We threw the packs down on it and began carving and stamping it into a shelf long enough and wide enough to accommodate the tents. It was a process that seemed to take forever and actually did take over an hour. We had only two ice axes to work with, Bob's and mine. Because the snow was only about eighteen inches deep, we could not simply carve back into the hillside, as we had at Slick Rock Creek; here that technique only encountered dirt. We were forced to build up the outside edge of the shelf by importing snow from elsewhere along the bulge. This would make a rather insecure sleeping arrangement in case the built-up snow decided to slip out during the night, but it was the only approach possible. Finally, at nine-thirty, the job was done. Now the tents went up in the darkness, the tail of one fastened to the ridgepole of the other, the two outside ends tied to ice axes driven as securely as possible into the bank. The knots had to be tied, and the stakes driven, mostly by feel. * We hoped they would hold. The rain had turned to snow, and a wind had come up.

There was a circular bare patch ten to fifteen feet in diameter nearby, caused by God knows what. We built a fire on it and cooked something resembling supper. Steve brought out a fifth of wine he had meant to keep for a summit celebration; we passed it around through the blizzard, and we all got slightly pie-eyed. Then we crawled into the tents, Steve and Bob into one, Harmon and I into the other. I took the outside edge because Harmon seemed to be afraid of it. In the close, dark, windless confines of the tent I rolled out my sleeping bag and snuggled into it. The blizzard howled down the slope outside. It was ten-thirty. I slept.

It was nearly twelve hours later when I awoke and still so dark in the tent that I thought at first my watch must have stopped. It was, however, not darkness of night but of the storm. I shivered into my old Navy-surplus parka and climbed out through the tent door. The sky was dropping something of a consistency between snow and hail; the flakes, or pellets, or whatever they were, blew past horizontally, propelled by a good thirty- to forty-mile-an-hour gale. Visibility was perhaps a hundred feet. I reminded myself, unsuccessfully, that it was June. Obviously, there was no sense in going further. We repacked wordlessly and started down the slope into the indistinctness of the storm.

A week later, Bob and I would try it again, alone this time. We would try it as a day trip, leaving Walla Walla at five-thirty in the morning, starting up the Frances Lake trail by eight, hoping to be back by dark. There would be no snow falling this trip, but there would be high clouds, intermittent drizzle, and thunderheads blooming on the southwestern horizon. Climbing beneath the spectacular face of Marble Point—a face we had not seen through the blizzard—we would make relatively short work of the long ladder of

*Like most backpackers I know, I rarely carry a flashlight. It adds weight to the pack and is usually unnecessary. City dwellers, used to nights under a layer of dirty air, simply do not realize how much light an unfiltered starry sky can provide—assuming, of course, that it isn't obscured by a blizzard.

switchbacks, the crazy back-and-forth-and-straight-up trail that Justice William O. Douglas described in his book *My Wilderness: The Pacific West* as "fit for neither man nor beast," gaining the ridge by a credible ten-thirty in the morning. There we would look down the far side, down eight hundred discouraging feet to Frances Lake, and then up again, up vast, barren piles of shale, discouraging and sere, to the crest of the Hurricane: Deadman Point, a pair of unnameds, and, higher and more barren than the others and crowned by those two impossible needles, Twin Peaks: our goal. We would gaze across at it, and we would gaze downward to Frances Lake, choked with drifting snow, and we would gaze southwestward to the thunderheads, and we would come to the reluctant conclusion that, again, it couldn't be done, not this trip, not yet. But there was an alternative, a way to salvage something from the trip, and we would take it. We would move southward along the ridge, over cornice and rock, half a mile to the base of the steep, five-hundred-foot final rise of Marble Point, and we would climb it. A tolerably exciting route-finding experience on good solid rock with plenty of holds; a short, snow-choked chimney; a broad and gentle summit snowfield; and finally the summit itself, wide and barren and high. We would explore the summit separately, an explore that would include, on my part, a short drop partway over the north face to a small ledge at the foot of an incredibly steep snowfield, just to see what it was like down there. Back on top, in the gathering electrical storm, I would experience, for the first time and, so far, also the last time, that sensation known as "the buzzing of the bees," in which all metal—particularly the metal parts of the ice axe, the adze, and the spike—hum and tingle and, yes, buzz like a gigantic and angry swarm. It is the signal of a proximal lightning strike and it means: Get off, fast! We would do so. The cliff descent and the glissade would be accomplished in what must have been record time. And later, down in the canyon, Bob would ask me, "What was the rush back there?"

"Didn't you hear the bees buzzing around your axe?"

"Well, yes, I did, but I didn't pay any attention to it. Why? What does that signify?" And then he would listen, his mouth dropping slowly open, as I told him that what it signified was that he had come perilously close to becoming a conduit for whatever electrical indigestion was growling around in the tummy of Marble Point just then. A few more seconds, and he would have been not just plain Bob, but Shish Ka Bob. . . .

But all this was still in the future, and the future was unknowable. The future, at that point, in that Frances Lake Divide blizzard, with total failure behind the four of us, didn't even *want* to be known. I didn't want to think about it. I didn't want to think at all. As I stumbled benumbed down the trail, I could only wonder helplessly what else I had to learn about snow.

IX

If anyone had asked me, this summer of 1964, why I continued to go to the Wallowas, I would quite frankly not have known how to answer.

The Wallowas certainly had not been *kind.* They had snowed on me, rained on me, and hailed on me; they had hidden behind fog and clouds; they had thrown avalanches at me; and they had come perilously close to electrocuting me. Worst of all, they had—with monotonous regularity—withheld their summits from me. For two years now I had been throwing myself liberally at the Wallowas and they had been responding by throwing me right back out again. I had failed on Sacajawea, failed on Twin, failed *even* to *begin* on the Matterhorn and Sawtooth. Since Pete's Point, in fact, I had failed at *every* goal I sought. There had been a few crumbs tossed to me in the way of alternate summits, to be sure—Deadman Point, Marble Point—but these did little to rectify the greater failures.

And yet I did not feel failure. Correction: I *felt* failure—felt it on every trip—but the feeling did not last. It slowed me down for a while each time, but each time it was eventually dissipated, to be replaced by, or possibly converted into, a kind of success. Already, by the summit of Marble Point, our dismal retreat from the Frances Lake Divide was undergoing this kind of metamorphosis. I did not then pretend to understand the process, and I do not now. I suspect that it has something to do with the simple victory of having *survived,* of having lived through the storm, of having faced danger and overcome it; but this is not all. This cannot be all. When one has merely survived something, he has no craving to go back, as I was now doing, time after time after time. There was something more than mere survival operating here. There was something else: a feeling—call it a feeling, though it is more than that—of rightness, of unity with the world and with yourself, a feeling that those who stay behind in what is (ridiculously) called the "real" world (the world that humanity has manufactured and wrapped around itself) cannot possibly comprehend. Everything contributes to this feeling, the failures as well as the successes. The failures perhaps *more* than the successes. For certainly the person who looks out of a warm window at the blowing snow and then turns the thermostat up another notch and goes back to a book can never know the essence of snow as I had felt it on the blizzard-swept summit ridge of Sacajawea, or in a tiny, very mortal tent someplace on the side of the Frances Lake Divide. The book and the house are a separation, and those who depend exclusively on them are always apart from the processes of the earth. We, for a time at least, had been one with them.

In answer to your question, no, I did not verbalize this at the time. Though I had wavered a bit after Sacajawea, I had executed a recovery; I once more considered myself primarily a climber— i.e., conqueror—and my failures were very real *at the time of failure.* It was only afterward, as I kept coming back for more and more punishment, that I realized that I might have to redefine my terms; that what I was calling "failure" was only incidental, and that the real purposes of each trip were being fully and beautifully realized. The problem was not that I was failing; the problem was that I did not understand the terms of success.

And all this (as you might have guessed) is a form of prelude to yet another failure. . . .

The Outing Club advisor, Mr. White, was also active in the Walla Walla First Congregational Church and had been instrumental in obtaining my job there for me. A slight, boyish-looking mathematics instructor in his late thirties, with one of the friendliest smiles I have ever run into, Conrad White had a background that can only be described as unusual. While growing up in Texas he had been something of a child prodigy on the piano; up to his mid-teens he had seemed slated for a concert career. Then he suddenly dropped the piano and entered theological training. After completing his ministerial studies, and just prior to his ordination, he came to the conclusion that the ministry did not suit him either; so that career also went out the window, and he went off to India to teach mathematics and physical science at a mission school near Madras. That lasted five years. Now he was back in the States and teaching mathematics at Whitman. Soon this too would end, and he would go to New York to edit textbooks for a large and prestigious publishing firm—an occupation in which he has remained, with minor changes, to this day.

In his capacity as a lay leader in the church, Conrad particularly enjoyed working with youth; and it was this enthusiasm of his that, in a roundabout sort of way, led us to be rained out of the Wallowas. He was scheduled to lead a United Church of Christ high school group into the range in early August for a week of mixed backpacking and theology, and he wanted to check the route out beforehand. He was planning to take Bill Meyers, the seventeen-year-old son of the church secretary, who bore a striking resemblance to Bob Lawrence at the same age; they intended to move fast, covering the entire week-long group route in just three days. Would I like to come along?

I did not need to be asked twice.

The clouds were gathering (as usual) when we left the car at Two Pan and started up the trail along the West Fork of the Lostine River. I paid little attention to the clouds. I had grown so used to entering the Wallowas under a cloud bank that this one did not seem at all out of place. Besides, how serious could it be? It was mid-July; a blizzard to match the one I had been through on Sacajawea, or even on the Frances Lake Divide, seemed preposterously unlikely. We would top no peaks, so lightning should not be a serious hazard. All we would get would be a little rain, and what harm could there be in that? We strode confidently forward.

The trail switchbacked gently upward through open forest, traversed a low-angle slope, and came out above the foaming river. Elkhorn Peak leaped massively into view, gray against gray of sky, above a muted white necklace of snow. We contoured, then climbed beside waterfalls. I was running well, body in tune, pack riding easily, feeling, as the commercials used to say, "like a healthy animal"; it was difficult to avoid comparisons with the one former time I had left a car at Two Pan and walked forth upon a Wallowa trail, the East Lostine trail instead of the west, that time, on my way as a rank novice to climb Eagle Cap. Everything had been new to me then: the feel of the pack, the smell of the trail and the sensation of it beneath my boots, the lay of the terrain and the scale of it, the taste of mountain water, and a thousand other things that slipped by me entirely because I simply did not know enough to look for them. I had bumbled forward, propelled more by enthusiasm than anything else, blissfully ignorant of the scope of the task I was attempting and carrying it through mostly by dint of sheer luck. Now all that had changed. I approached this trip not in ignorance but with a reasonable amount of experience under the bellyband of my pack. I had now spent a total of thirty-three days in the Pacific Northwest wilderness, spread over thirteen separate trips, two-thirds of them in the Wallowas. I had toiled my way to ten summits, seven of those ten in the Wallowas; I had labored more than one-hundred-thirty miles beneath a backpack, not counting day hikes and side trips. Three trips had been in the winter; four, if you counted the Frances Lake Divide. I wasn't ready to tackle Mt. Mc-Kinley yet, but I was aware that I wasn't ready, and that awareness was an achievement in itself. It showed that the experience was doing some good. And there were other, less subtle ways that this showed, too. No longer, for instance, was each step a revelation; I knew the smell of the dust and the taste of the water, I knew the feel of the pack, I knew how I was going to have to pace myself to make the six miles of Minam Lake and still have some energy left. This loss of innocence was sad, in a way, but it did have its compensations. There was confidence and there was an easy familiarity with the trail, even though this particular trail was one I had not seen before. My backpack was becoming part of me, and the wilderness was becoming home.

With loss of innocence, it is often said, goes loss of wonder. But this is not so, or at least it had not been for me. As a beginner, I had wondered about *everything;* each step, as I have said, was a revelation. This tended to spread the sense of wonder rather thin. Now, released from its step-by-step concentration, wonder was free to bunch and soar, coming to rest in previously unexpected places. Not on the shape of a peak but on the *why* behind that shape; not on the form of a lake but on the fact of its presence. And not on the nameless uniformity of the forest as scenery but on the unnameable diversity of the forest as life.

And it was with these thoughts easing through my receptive brain that I came around a long corner by the dancing river and found there the green meadows at the mouth of Copper Creek.

These meadows do not appear on any map. They are too small for mapping, being no more than tiny islands of grass in the midst of the tall forest; the largest covers scarcely an acre. Through them the West Lostine loops in a series of still, deep, and utterly transparent pools, the water so clear as to seem disembodied. Around, at a respectful distance, stand the mountains; one perfectly formed granite pyramid, in front of and a little apart from the mass, hovers quietly over the scene like a respectful father. It is a place of simple beauty and great peace.

We stood awhile by the river, savoring that beauty and that peace. I cannot speak for the others, but on my part the desire for new country had almost entirely abated. I could have stayed perpetually in those meadows. This was a new sensation for me. Always before I had been propelled by a need to see what was around the next corner, beyond the next line of trees, over the next hill. . . . and now this was no longer true. The Copper-Lostine Meadows had seduced me, had drugged me as surely and as thoroughly as the poppy fields of Oz had drugged Dorothy, and when it came time to move on up the long hill beyond the meadows, I did so with great reluctance, stopping often to look back over my shoulder and completely ignoring the danger that in doing so I might risk being turned into a pillar of salt. Then a corner hid them, and I resolutely turned my attention back toward what was to come.

What this might be was still uncertain. Though the clouds had advanced no further, they had not retreated either, and the air was mildly chilly even in the direct rays of the weakened, dissolute sun. We ate lunch in a small clearing by a stream, glad for the presence of sun-warmed granite on which to lie back and soak up a little extra heat—in mid-July! For a long time after lunch we moved through the flat upper canyon, the river making great sweeping meanders beside us, the dark molar shape of Brown Mountain looming to starboard. Just past two-thirty we climbed a small grassy rise and came to a wide sheet of water, gray under a gray sky, lapping a far shore that rose into unnamed, flat-topped crags beneath thunderheads. Minam Lake.

My first reaction, unaccountably, was disappointment: *You mean we're here already?* My second reaction was also disappointment, but for another reason. Minam Lake has been artificially raised, and it suffers from drawdown. No one had warned me about this. It was like marrying a beautiful and demure girl and finding out, on the wedding night, that she had once worked as a prostitute. The drawdown was not terribly apparent, but it was terribly *there*.

Halfway along the shore, in a grove of trees bordering a wide, muddy, and not-quite-natural beach, we shed our packs. We had a full six hours of daylight left, and we would use it for further exploration, including—we hoped—a visit to the source of the Minam River. But first it would be a good idea to put up the tents. The rain would not hold off forever; and if it started while we were away, it would be gratifying to have a nice, dry, already-pitched shelter to come back to.

I was getting quite adept at handling my little two-man mountain tent by now, and it went up quickly. The process runs something like this: First, locate a suitable flat spot (or make one, if you are on a mountainside in a snowbank) and clear it of twigs, pine cones, and the most obvious rocks. Untie the tent from its home on the pack frame (just beneath the bag) and roll it out. If there is a slight slant to your flat spot, orient the tent so that you will be sleeping with your head uphill, unless there is a wind blowing, in which case you will want to face the tent door into the wind; otherwise the tent will flap all night like a gigantic bird and keep you miserably awake, wondering when it is all going to come down around your ears. Hunt through your pack for your tent pegs (I carry eight-inch steel spikes, wrapped in an old sock; some people prefer aluminum, or wood precarved at home) and pin down the four corners of the flat tent, stretching it taut. Locate a suitable anchor point to the rear, place the *short* aluminum pole under the rear eave, and tie the rear anchor line. Untelescope the *long* aluminum pole, feel around inside the collapsed vestibule until you locate the front eave, socket the pole in it, and raise the front end of the tent. Tie the front anchor line, making sure to get plenty of downbearing on that front pole so it will stay upright. Place the three remaining pegs, one in the center of each long side, one at the front of the vestibule. As a final, strictly optional touch, search around for a springy little branch slightly longer than the tent is wide; hook one end of the branch through one of the two loops located halfway up the sides of the tent at midpoint, lay it across the ridgepole, and hook the other end through the matching loop on the other side. This will pull the sides of the tent up and out and greatly increase the room you have to move about within—to say nothing of improving its stability in the face of whatever winds may blow.

Unzip the door and crawl inside.

With Bill Meyers helping me—he was going to sleep there, too— the job went rapidly and without a hitch. We threw our packs inside, zipped down the door, and went to see how Mr. White was faring. Not so well. As an experiment, and to see if it would be possible to lighten the loads his youth-campers would be carrying, he had brought no tent, only a nine-foot-by-twelve-foot plastic drop cloth and twenty yards or so of nylon line. Using these alone, he was attempting to rig an adequate shelter. He had hoped to find a pair of trees about ten feet apart so that a level line tied between them might serve as his ridgeline, but no such setup was possible in the grove we had chosen. So he had run his ridgeline from a loop tied four feet up the trunk of a tree, down to a point on the ground about twelve feet away, and back up to another tree beside the first. He placed the drop cloth over these. It migrated down them and bunched at the bottom. He pulled it back up and tied it down, pulling it taut between pegs driven into the ground. The tie-down process itself posed problems: The drop cloth had no grommets through which to pass lines. But Mr. White had been prepared for this, and his solution was ingenious. He looked for and found a number of rounded stones approximately the size of a child's fist; one of these was placed behind the plastic at each tie-down point, and the plastic was twisted around it, forming a thin, many-layered neck behind a hard knob. The tie-down line went around the neck, then to the tent peg. Gradually, from the billowing plastic, something resembling a shelter began to emerge. It bore an unlikely resemblance to a Dutch Colonial roof following a tornado. Mr. White eyed it critically.

"I think my campers had better carry tents," he said.

Well, at least it would keep the rain out. Maybe. He put his pack inside, wrapping it in the "floor"—the flapping leftovers of drop cloth beyond the tie-downs, lapped inward instead of outward so that they could act as ground protection. Under the still-threatening but not-yet-delivering skies, we moved southward out of camp toward what the map said was the Minam's source—a lake called Blue, a mile away, at the base of those flat-topped crags we had noticed as soon as we reached Minam Lake.

We passed the trail we would take the next day, angling steeply off to the left to begin its switchbacking climb toward Lower Horton Pass, a thousand feet above. We rounded the south end of the lake, crossing beside it on a small earth-fill dam. That would be the source of the drawdown. Water seeped under the dam, trickling and splashing down into the great gulf at the head of the Minam Canyon. We were moving upward through the forest beyond the lake, angling out over the canyon head, before the significance of that trickle struck me. Minam Lake drains principally from the *north*, forming the West Lostine River. But quite obviously it also drained to the *south*. The water going that way would end up in the main stem of the Minam River. So Minam Lake fed two major Wallowa Mountain streams, the Lostine and the Minam; and since both were tributaries of the Wallowa River itself, the land between them was entirely surrounded by water. *We were on an island!*

The trail climbed gradually through timber, with occasional views opening expansively southward over the canyon toward the back side of Eagle Cap and, beyond, the sharp gray spire of Jackson Peak. It leveled out briefly, then turned to the right. Straight up the fall line. Fortunately, this stretch of trail was short, and very soon we were moving across level ground through widely spaced large trees to the edge of Blue Lake. The trail reached the water's edge just where the outlet stream left it; for a while, we simply stood quietly in the cool and moving sunlight, the broad lake at our feet, watching the Minam being born.

Eventually we separated, moving individually, each with his own thoughts, beside the lapping water. The lake filled practically its entire cirque, and to walk beside it at any point save the outer rim was to pick one's way at the bottom of steep talus. The flat-topped crags, close at hand now, hung over steep snowfields with their feet in the far end of the lake. The water was incredibly blue, even under these gray and threatening skies. It seemed very deep.

I sat on a gray stone by the blue water, overstaying my time away from the others and knowing it, lingering anyway, unwilling yet to leave. For the second time that day, the idea had come upon me that *here I could stay forever.* As in the Copper-Lostine Meadows, the urge to explore, to climb, to conquer, to catch up with the horizon, seemed to waver and fade and finally to vanish altogether. I felt acutely alive and utterly at peace. And I began to sense that somehow my approach to the mountains would never again be as it had been. I would climb again, yes; I would seek summits and chase horizons. These would remain goals. But they would no longer be the *only* goals. Perhaps they never had been; perhaps it was just that I was only now realizing it. Earlier, my great enthusiasm for adventure was getting in the way, but now that this enthusiasm had been tempered and subdued by experience, it was ready to begin falling into balance with other things; with wholeness and restfulness and peace.

I got up from my stone. It was time to leave, and the others would be waiting. Slowly, each step a pure joy, I moved back along the lakeshore. I did not look back. And this time, unlike the seduction practiced on me by the Copper-Lostine Meadows, the feeling detached itself from the place and came with me. It made leaving easier. I walked peacefully down the trail toward camp, in tune even with the gathering rain.

The rain began as we crossed the small dam at the south end of Minam Lake and rounded the corner onto the east shore—a few large drops puffing the dust, then a machine gun spattering that sent us diving for the trees, finally a steady gray wetness that could be described as either a light rain or a heavy drizzle. This last showed signs of becoming permanent. We wandered about in our gray grove, looking out over the gray lake. From time to time the clouds would lift far enough to see the mountains beyond the water, but for the most part we seemed locked in the center of a primal wetness, our trees and tents and the near edge of the lake our only anchors on reality. We ate a wet supper and went unusually early to bed. At least it was dry in the tent. I slept lightly; every now and again I would wake to the sound of rain rattling on the nylon shell of the tent. A cozy sound. But how was Mr. White faring?

Mr. White was not faring so well. Mr. White was, in fact, spending a rather difficult night. Because his shelter was open at both ends, the wind funneled through it, bringing with it the rain, a fine cold spray misting over him as if from an atomizer. Moisture from his breath condensed on the inside of the plastic, gathering there and dripping onto him; he was, in effect, creating his own private rainstorm *inside* the shelter. The plastic billowed and snapped, creaked and tore. Water puddled beside it and seeped under it. Mr. White, as he said later, was never so glad to see daylight as he was on the following morning.

But it was still raining—a dark rain, drifting miserably from heavy, low-hanging clouds. We broke camp damply, wrapping everything that had managed to remain dry overnight in plastic and in the process, of course, distributing the moisture evenly from the wet things to the dry. Still, nothing seemed irredeemably soaked, and within my plastic rain gear I was comfortable enough. And the cool, moist air was certainly invigorating. We had an 8,400-foot pass in front of us, up a thousand feet and back down again in less than three miles. Would you rather do that in the heat of an August afternoon?

We began. The trail lifted through rain into fog, now diving into clumps of timber, now crossing open, stony slopes from which, sans clouds, the view must have been magnificent. Now and again windows would open in the clouds, framing Brown Mountain or the crags above Blue Lake or offering a long, tunneled view of a section of the floor of the Minam Canyon. The trail switchbacked, crossing snowfields, contouring a small, dark basin above a pond. There were rock outcrops and hanging gardens. There was a long stony slope. There was rain. Vision closed down to twenty feet.

We crossed the pass.

I had been hoping for a view from that pass, but of course we didn't get one; only fog and clouds, and more fog and clouds.

Somewhere down there was Mirror Lake and Upper Lake and beyond them the rest of the lakes of the Lake Basin, blue under gray cliffs, sparkling among mountains. Somewhere—on another day. Today there were only fog and clouds. Today we would have to practically step into one of the lakes before we could see it. And even then it might be difficult to tell where air stopped and lake began. This stuff we were breathing was very nearly thick enough to require the use of an aqualung.

We started down.

Almost at once we entered the flowers—great steep sweeping fields of flowers, heather mostly, turning the mountainside pink in all directions as far as the fog would let us see. The trail tacked through heather. There were small outcrops of white stone; there were lacy waterfalls trailing over steep smooth rock, the heather parting for them as evenly as if some gardener had trimmed it. The water was sweet. It seemed a paradise parkland, a garden only slightly less perfect than Eden, and absolutely nothing else in these mountains—and certainly nothing on the Minam side of the pass— had prepared me for it. I moved slowly downward, savoring each blossom, each white stream. Occasional breaks in the fog allowed glimpses downhill across flowers to the near end of Upper Lake, shining like pewter, its far end a mist and a vagueness. I was almost grateful for that vagueness. Without it, would I have noticed the flowers? Or would I have been too busy with mountains and lakes and things at unreachable distances to notice the perfection at my feet?

All too soon we came down out of heather heaven into the more normal meadows at the edge of Upper Lake. It was raining harder now; my pants had soaked through and were clinging to my thighs. And there was no shelter in sight, not even a tree. Mr. White strode angrily in the lead, across a bog that sucked at our boots, toward the southward, cliff-ringed side of Mirror Lake. We were headed, at my request, toward a rocky little peninsula jutting out from those south-side cliffs—my first-ever camp in the Wallowas, back in the Eagle Cap days, back in sixty-one.

I was going home.

The lone tree on the point gave scant shelter, but it was better than nothing. Mr. White and Bill crowded under it while I searched the ground nearby for pieces of memories. There was not much to find. I could remember where each of us on that first trip had slept, but there was no sign to prove me right. Down by the lake, black smoke-stain showed faintly where we had built our fire. The spring we had cleaned on my first trip into the mountains was still running, though it needed cleaning again; the pool had filled with silt to within half an inch of the overflow slot we had so painstakingly constructed. When I leaned over it, the rain ran down my neck. I scooped out silt with my hands, waited for the water to clear, then drank. And then it was time to go.

We hurried northward, the rain in our faces, around the end of the lake toward a tight, dry little grove on the north side where we could eat lunch without drinking it at the same time.

It was while we were eating lunch that we decided to leave.

The decision was not a difficult one. We were wedged, the three of us, between two tree trunks barely three feet apart, crowded together, trying desperately to stay dry while the rain pat-patted around us. We were not succeeding. Stray raindrops were penetrating even through the tight, interwoven roof of branches and branchlets and needles over us. Worse, the relatively small raindrops would trickle together among the high branches, conglomerate into one large drop, and then descend like liquid Ping Pong balls onto our foreheads, our hands, our hats, or the backs of our necks. "Hey, fearless leader," I grinned at Mr. White, "this damn tree leaks." Churchman White was not amused. "Watch your language, young man," he snapped. Of the three of us, he had suffered the worst. His raincoat had lost both sleeves; his pack was soaked clear down to the lunch food. And he was justifiably worried about spending another night in the rain with only his now somewhat battered plastic drop cloth for a shelter. Anyway, we had done what we came to do. By the time we reached the car, somewhere down the East Lostine Canyon, we would have covered the three principal legs of his planned youth-camp route. He would have enough information to choose his campsites wisely—or at least, if he didn't have that information now, he never would have it. So when he suggested retreating in the face of the rain, Bill and I didn't argue with him. I suppose it would have been possible to talk him into staying, had one of us offered to trade places with him for the night, sleeping under the plastic while he took one of the two spaces in the tent. But neither of us so offered. We were wet, too, and the thought of a warm dry car—and a warm dry bed for the night—was not unwelcome.

We started out.

And now, perversely, the rain stopped. The clouds lifted, the weak sun filtered through, and we could *see*: Mirror Lake like a blue steel, burnished plate; and the gray peaks around it; and the black trees on the far shore; and, behind us, the great sweep of pink meadow dropping down from Lower Horton Pass. Was it an omen? Briefly, we hesitated. But even as we watched, clouds began to filter back over the pass. Far down the long, level canyon of the East Lostine a squall was dancing. Better not to trust anything to change. Better to continue homeward.

We dropped down the granite slope at the head of the canyon. A cold wind had come up, heavy with moisture; the squall seemed to have moved closer. A few drops hit, heavy and widely scattered, like the beginning of yesterday's storm by Minam Lake, only this time there was no dust to puff up. A drizzle mist drifted down, then lifted. There was a moment of hesitation, a single throb of the earth's great secret heart. . . .

Then the heavens opened, and it poured.

It rained buckets and barrels; it rained sheets and petticoats; it rained cats and dogs and Kilkenny kennels. The rain fell like a river, not in drops but in torrents, filling the air so thickly that it seemed almost as if to breathe would be to drown. The trail was slippery, and the treads of our boots were clogged with mud. We slipped and slid; we wriggled and squished. We ran. It rained. The minutes and the miles sogged by, but the downpour did not diminish. Perhaps it was good for forty days and forty nights. And never an ark in sight. We came to the bank of the swollen Lostine, at the ford just above Lost Lake, where the trail plunges into knee-deep water for thirty or forty feet and then climbs out on the far side. "We wade here," I said, kneeling to my bootlace. "Not on your life," said Mr. White. "Not in this stuff." He struck off rapidly through the trailless meadows on the east bank of the river, heading downstream in the rain. Bill followed. I retied my boot and hurried after them. It seemed to me that we were so wet already that a little extra wouldn't hurt, but on the other hand, why argue? We strode rapidly beside Lost Lake, on smooth, very narrow meadows tucked in between the lake and the canyon wall. The meadows were soggy. We passed a tent, buttoned up tight; perhaps there were people inside, waiting out the storm, but we didn't take the time to find out. At the foot of the lake, logs tumbled like jackstraws in the path of the river offered both an explanation of the lake's presence and a bridge to the far shore. We went across, balancing carefully on the wet, slippery roundness of the long-dead trunks. Soon we were back on the trail among tall trees that filtered the downpour to a drizzle. For the first time since leaving Mirror Lake Mr. White paused, grinning back at us from under his dripping hat brim. "Who said we'd have to wade?" he asked; and then, more seriously, "I'm glad we went that way. I wanted to see what those meadows looked like; they're going to be our last night's camp." "It's a good group camp," I said. "There were girl scouts there my first trip this way." I had known they were girl scouts because we had met a packer at the one-mile marker, while I was resting from my first big wrestling match with mountain distance. Bob Lawrence had asked him whom we might run into further up the trail. I could remember each drawled, exquisite inflection of his answer. There was a Walla Walla College biology class at Mirror Lake; he was provisioning a group of fishermen at Moccasin; and he'd heard tell that a large contingent of Portland Mazamas—a climbing club—were due in that weekend. Then there were the girl scouts at Lost Lake. And he had chuckled, looking us over, one by one. "You boys," he had said, "are goin' to have a hard time gettin' by there. . . ."

For a moment only the packer's face rose up in my mind; then the rain washed it away. Down the trail we fled, down the last two miles with the wet brush snatching at our legs as we passed, down toward the car and dryness and a chance to go home.

X

In August, a few weeks after the Great Lostine Rainstorm, I took my cousin Craig Stewart—then sixteen—for an overnight hike into the northern Blue Mountains. On something called the Burnt Cabin Trail we dropped some three thousand feet into the canyon of the South Fork of the Walla Walla River, crossed the river on a "bridge" consisting of a large log hewed flat on top, and turned east, up-canyon toward the Wenaha country. Some three miles up the canyon there was supposed to be a trail leading up the north rim, to a place called Table Spring, in the heart of the wilderness plateau between the north and south forks of the Walla Walla. We never found the trail. Whether we passed it by or simply never reached it was impossible to tell. We spent the night in the canyon and walked out the next day. Chalk up another failure.

In early September, in an ancient Plymouth I had owned since June, my fifteen-year-old brother, Jack, and I sallied forth on a long, celebration-of-youth trek south through central Oregon to the town of Klamath Falls, just north of the California border, where we spent nearly a week with Larry Chitwood. There were caves in the nearby Lava Beds; there were scrambles on weird pinnacles above Tule Lake. The high point of the trip, in more ways than one, was to be an eight-man ascent of Mt. Shasta, a 14,161-foot volcano just over the line in California. This turned out to be not so much a climb as a comedy, at least as it is looked back upon. At the time it didn't seem so funny. We left supper and most of breakfast in

Klamath Falls. The campsite Larry had picked as a takeoff point from the cars to the summit turned out to be a borrow pit for the County Roads Department. We left the lunch at Lake Helen, a snowfield at about the ten-thousand-foot level on the mountain. Altitude sickness, strongly exacerbated by our lack of food over the past twenty-four hours, made each step above the infamous Red Banks a major effort, as a part of the mountain named Misery Hill lived enthusiastically up to its reputation. We struggled through sun cups two to three feet deep. Just below the crest of Misery Hill, the four of us who were still climbing—Larry, Jack, me, and Larry's brother Don—shared the only sustenance we had taken all day. Two antacid tablets. A short distance later, a quarter mile from the summit and two hundred feet below it, we turned back. It seemed a miracle that we had gotten that far, even, and we probably would not have done so had not each of us in that remaining four had a brother along he had to prove something to. Back at Lake Helen we found that the four who had turned back previously had eaten nearly all the lunch. The cars had disappeared in the dusk, and it took us nearly half an hour of scrambling tiredly about the side of the mountain in the gathering darkness to locate them. By that time I no longer cared. I was ready to simply sit down where I was and let whatever it was that would happen, happen. We returned, somehow, to Klamath Falls. Add still another failure to the board.

Back to school, my fifth and last year at Whitman, rolling around through classes and meetings and Outing Club activities, rolling through winter to lilac-heavy spring. We failed to reach Griffen Peak. My ancient Plymouth died and was replaced by an even older Kaiser. Outing Club president Bruce Foote fell in the river at Palouse Falls. An early May Blue Mountains hike turned into an aimless drive on endless muddy roads, seeking an apparently nonexistent trail. Back in town, I walked among flowering trees, thinking of A. E. Housman's "The Chestnut Casts His Flambeaux":

> There's one spoilt spring to scant our mortal lot,
> One season ruined of our little store:
> May will be fine next year, as like as not—
> Ah, yes! But then we shall be twenty-four.

Was I ready to leave college? Had I grown up enough, and were the mountains helping?

As its final activity of the year, the Outing Club planned a mountain climb. Guided by my constant and not-so-subtle prodding, the club agreed to make that climb in the Wallowas. Our goal was Joseph Peak, a great broad precipitous hump of a mountain, 9,600 feet tall, that forms most of the north wall of the range near the town of Joseph. The crest of this vast pile stretches for nearly eight miles, from the Wallowa Canyon to the Hurricane; its north face forms a vertical wall four miles broad and nearly a mile high. We had no plans to get out on that north face: We would tackle the mountain from the south, instead, through BC Basin. I had never seen BC Basin, but the topographic map said it should be easier. So did the ranger I wrote to in Joseph. Well, we would see.

On the evening of Friday, May 14, seven of us piled into two cars and drove the ninety miles from Walla Walla to a Boy Scout camp on Wallowa Lake where we had arranged to spend the night. A full moon rode a perfect sky over Bonneville Peak. In the lodge we slept on tables and benches, there being no mattresses of any kind about. By five in the morning we were all stiffly awake and anxious to be moving. Our new advisor, Dr. Jim Todd of the chemistry department, was not interested in summits; he would go for a walk in the woods by himself, instead. He said good-bye to us, and we started.

There is an old, exceedingly unmaintained trail up BC Creek. Where it existed, we followed it. Where it didn't exist, we beat brush or made our way around dense little groves of trees. The world was fresh and gray in the gathering light. We crossed rockslides, stretching uphill out of sight into the gloom. Patches of snow appeared, then great sweeping fields of it. The gray of morning resolved itself into the blue and white and green of glorious day.

At perhaps seven-thirty we came to a great, steep, snow-filled couloir, sweeping down the mountain from distant ridge to foaming creek. The trail was obliterated. The three of us who were experienced held a small conference. Would this couloir be a proper route to the ridge? We decided to try it. Tom Stanlick, an enthusiastic and knowledgeable sophomore, took the lead. Shortly behind him

came freshman Jim Manley, a product of the Spokane Moun-
taineers training classes. I lagged in the rear, climbing with a girl
named Pat, in whom I had a mild interest. It turned out to be for-
tunate that I so lagged. Several hundred feet up the slope, fifty feet
or so ahead of where Pat and I were climbing, Diana Duncan—the
only other girl in the party—lost her footing and went down. The
high-angled, crusty snow received her but refused to hold her. She
began speeding helplessly downhill.

Tom and I had given everyone brief verbal instructions in how to
use your ice axe to stop yourself, but Diana had evidently not
understood. The secret of success in a self-arrest is to get the axe
under your chest, so that the entire weight of your upper body may
be brought to bear on the pick as you drive it into the snow to act as
a brake. Diana had caught the part about driving the pick into the
snow, but she hadn't comprehended the need for weight on the axe
handle. Arms outstretched, she scratched the snow with her axe as
far as she could reach above her head. It had little or no effect. She
gathered speed rapidly. Hundreds of feet below, the creek waited.

My reaction, I am proud to say, was almost instantaneous. I was
on my way as soon as I saw that Diana could not stop herself. Running horizontally across the slope, I crouched in her path, my axe in
arrest position. She hurtled toward me. I caught the soles of her
boots on the shaft of my axe and and threw myself into a proper
arrest position across axe and feet together, my cheek scraping the
snow beside her knees. She knocked me from my stance. For a
moment her momentum, and the sudden thrust as part of it trans-
ferred to me, threatened to put us both in the creek; then my axe bit
the snow and held. We slowed and stopped.

A short distance beyond, the couloir opened to the left and there
was a small level patch above trees. For more than an hour, while
the sun climbed and the summit receded, Tom and I used that spot
as a classroom, sending the two women and the one inexperienced
man down the slope over and over until we were satisfied that each
one of them could handle a self-arrest well enough to avoid
disasters like the one that had almost occurred. Then we roped up.
I took the lead on one rope, Tom on the other; we tied the girls into

the middle. Fastened firmly between me and Jim Manley, Diana visibly relaxed. We were ready to start climbing again.

But now the sun was high, and the couloir, once looked upon as a shortcut to the ridge, seemed to grow until it stretched infinitely before us. We toiled our way upward, winding back and forth across the steep, broadening face. Rest stops came at decreasing intervals. Jim and I, reveling in the luxury of having experienced men on both ends of the rope, began changing the lead every fifty paces. Tom, leading a rope with two inexperienced climbers on it, could not do this. He started to tire. Seeking easier ground, he took to the rocks beside the snow. That lasted about a hundred feet. Back on the snow, his rope fell further and further behind. The hands of my watch swept past noon. The mountain continued.

At twelve-thirty we stopped on a broad pile of rocks and ate lunch.

At one-thirty we came at last to the ridge. Humped stone and cornices and krummholz. We made for the nearest hump. It wasn't the summit—the summit was still a thousand feet above us, looming over us, there to the west—but it would have to do. We weren't going any further. We unroped and settled down to enjoy the view, which was magnificent. To the north, the broad, snow-streaked North Face plunged four thousand feet straight down to blue and distant plains. Our ridge curved downward to the east and dove into Wallowa Lake, the rumpled blue sheet of its surface thrusting four miles out onto the plain between twin moraines so new and raw-looking—from this altitude—that they might have been piled up yesterday. Beyond the lake, far beyond, rose the hazy Seven Devils Mountains in distant Idaho. And to the south, back the way we had come, lay the tumbled and snowy ridges of the Wallowas.

Aneroid Mountain leaped up, and Pete's Point, and Bonneville. At the head of the Wallowa Canyon, the shining white pyramid of Cusick Mountain split the blue and distant sky. Sacajawea peered, magnificent and close, through a gap in the Hurwal Divide. And cupping over it all, like a second sky, was a deep and living silence. It wasn't the Pete's Point silence, but it was something close to it. It was huge.

After a while I detached myself from the group and went west, down our hump and along the connecting ridge to the next hump, some three hundred feet distant. There were just too damn many people; even six was too many. I wanted to be alone, alone with myself and the mountain and the silence. But it was not to be. I had been there no more than ten minutes when Pat joined me, climbing quietly up beside me to sit down and gaze, as I was doing, over the distant plains. As I have said, I was mildly interested in Pat. At that moment I began to be uninterested. I said nothing, but my thoughts were churning. My god, woman—don't you recognize worship when you see it? There are times for sharing silence, but this is not one of them. Go away! But of course she didn't. The deep silence became shallow and uncomfortable. I was genuinely glad when we were hailed from the other knob and told it was time to go.

The descent was slow. The girls were afraid to glissade; Jim Manley and I stayed with them, helping them gradually down, while the others went ahead. Eventually we worked out a leap-frogging method of descent, Jim sliding fifty feet past us down the hill, waiting for the girls and helping them stop, then staying with them while I slid to them and beyond another fifty feet, to where I could take my turn as a backstop. It was tedious but faster than walking. After an hour or so we reached the trail. The lodge was not far beyond.

The drive home settled quickly into moodiness. Behind the wheel of my Kaiser I brooded, cursing the car around corners. Joseph had been another goddamned failure! A complete failure, a failure with the dull thud of totality. Not only had the summit not been obtained, but the damn mountain had given me nothing to take its place—no Copper-Lostine Meadows, no Blue Lakes, no new insights into mountain structure, nothing. Yet, to be fair, it wasn't entirely the fault of the mountain; much of that rested with the people around me, in my car and behind me in Jim Todd's Volkswagen. Not in their conduct—it was no different from mine—but in their numbers. I had learned something from this trip, after all. I had learned that a large group cannot enter the wilderness. A large group takes a part of civilization with it—the crowded part, the part wilderness is largely an escape *from*. Well, it wouldn't happen again, not to me.

It is significant to note here that every trip I took into the Wallowas after this was with but a single companion.

Back to Walla Walla and to graduation. Whitman became history. I would enter graduate school at Washington State University in the fall.

I went home to Pullman.

I got a job as a janitor at the university.

I tried, without success, to renew high school friendships.

I stared for long hours at maps of the route to Cusick Mountain.

XI

During my high school years, when I had not yet been to the Wallowas, my visual image of the range was based primarily on a single picture. I had seen it first as a photograph in a book, then as an eight-by-ten color print used as a gas station promotional give-away, and finally as a drawing (based on the photograph) appearing on the cover of the same gasoline company's road map. The scene: a timbered valley, with a long ribbed ridge of stone jutting up behind it. Halfway along, the ridge rose and fell in a sharp little pyramid of a peak not unlike the head of a crouching lion.

In the foreground, high above the valley, a pack train picked its way carefully through slanting green meadows.

All the way in to Eagle Cap and back out again, I had carried the image of that meadow and that valley and that leonine ridge right at the front of my mind. I had looked for it at each turn of the trail, sought its image in each new ridge that came into view, looked over my shoulder for it in case I had happened to miss it the first time around. I remained disappointed. The lion did not roar.

I looked for it again on the way to Pete's Point the following year. But I did not see it there, either.

I did not see it on my two trips to the Hurricane; I did not see it on the Frances Lake Divide or around Minam Lake. Most recently, I had not seen it on Joseph Mountain. But by this time I no longer much cared. I had become familiar with the Wallowas, had grown into them almost like a second skin, and this familiarity had produced not contempt, as in the old adage, but contentment and the beginning of an understanding of what wilderness and the mountains were all about; therefore, what *I* must be all about. It was this understanding, I am now certain, that had surfaced so dramatically in the Copper-Lostine Meadows and at Blue Lake. The fact was that now, set down in any part of the Wallowas, new or old, I could feel comfortably at home. And I no longer needed the false familiarity of a scene in a photograph to feel as if I knew the country around me.

Still, I couldn't help wondering a little. Where *was* that sphinx and its valley? In the south, where I had never been? Far in the west, near China Cap? Or had I already seen it and simply not recognized it? This last was at least a possibility. If I had learned anything in the Wallowas, I had learned that there is always much new to see in what you have already seen. But this same knowledge made the search for the photograph scene even less important. A photograph is dead and frozen, but the Wallowas are alive. While in the Wallowas I should be enjoying that aliveness, not looking for displaced pieces of somebody else's distant past.

And so the meadow and the valley and the leonine ridge migrated slowly backward through my mind till they reached the far end of my consciousness, and there they hovered, shelved and buried and not quite forgotten, waiting. . . .

July 3, 1965. The Safeway market in Enterprise had the cheapest form of background music available—a radio, tuned to a local station and playing softly. Just now, though, what it was playing was not music. Halfway down the aisle between cheese and mosquito repellent, Ed Hicks and I stopped to listen.

". . . *Hobo Lake, frozen over. Horseshoe Lake, clear. Ice Lake, frozen over. Jewett Lake, frozen over. John Henry Lake, pack ice, some clear areas. Little Frazier Lake, frozen over. Little Storm Lake, pack ice. Looking Glass Lake* . . ."

"Sounds cold," said Ed.

"Shh!" I held up a finger, gesturing for silence. The list droned on, through familiar and not-so-familiar names. Mirror was covered with pack ice. Moccasin was partly clear. Steamboat. . . . I listened for the name "Frazier Lake" but did not hear it. Perhaps its condition had already been announced before we came in. The report concluded, *"Most trails above seven thousand feet still snowed in. This has been your KWVR Lakes Report. Stay tuned for. . . ."* I stopped listening. We moved toward the check-out stand.

"You didn't tell me," said Ed, "that we'd have to sleep in the snow."

"I didn't know," I answered defensively. "Anyway, maybe we won't." I frowned, trying to remember the map, which I had left in Pullman. Let's see: Summit of Cusick about 9,600; I had figured on a 2,500-foot ascent above Frazier, that must mean the lake is at 7,100 feet. Where did that fit into the list? Trails above 7,000 feet mostly snowed in. . . . "It's all right," I grinned at Ed, as we loaded the groceries into the car. "The trail should be clear most of the way. And we can camp a little below the lake if we have to." I slipped behind the wheel and turned the key. Under high clouds, with the mountains looming neck-craning thousands of feet above us, we headed for the West Fork of the Wallowa and the trailhead.

The light was gray in the parking lot as we strapped on our packs and headed for the West Fork trail. Not a dawn gray, but a pre-storm gray, gentle but somehow ominous. I watched Ed somewhat anxiously as we pulled up the first long switchbacks and swung around the corner above the river. How would he take the rain? More importantly, how would he take the distance? *Would* he take the distance? I had no way of knowing; we would just have to wait and see.

I had known Ed barely two weeks. In the course of what had turned out to be futile attempts to renew high school acquaint-anceships, I had paid a call on an old friend and found Ed rooming with him. Ed went in for track, tumbling, and similar individually competitive sports. He was six feet tall, rather carelessly muscled, and he would try anything once. Mountain climbing? "Why not?" he answered.

I borrowed an extra pack and showed him how to load it. We went.

By the time we passed the junction with the Ice Lake trail, three miles in, my doubts about Ed had mostly vanished. He was moving strongly, in good humor, wearing the pack as if it were built onto him. We had a long way to go yet, of course—six more miles, if we went all the way to Frazier Lake—but we appeared likely to make it. I took Ed's picture against the rugged, gray-black shoulder of Craig Mountain. We went on.

At six miles, the trail from the Lake Basin came swinging down the hill to the right, the polished hill that had once held an icefall as the Lake Basin glacier came tumbling down to join the valley glacier in the West Fork. I pointed out the signs to Ed—the smooth curve of the lip, the steep, even sides of the mouth of the basin, the scratched boulders at our feet. I grew somewhat prideful, once more, in my ability to read these signs. Fortunately, Ed didn't seem to mind. I took his picture against Craig Mountain again. The peak had changed shape; the shoulder that had seemed so huge and impregnable earlier was now dwarfed into insignificance by the abrupt tilted pyramid of the summit, jutting up from the middle of its long ridge. There is an easy side to Craig, but it doesn't show from this angle. Ed was properly impressed and said he hoped our mountain didn't look like *that*. I assured him we would see in a few minutes.

Less than half a mile further, the rain began. This was not the brutal kamikaze rain of the Lostine; this was a gentle rain, falling easily and gracefully from the sky, stroking the plants, caressing rather than pounding the soil. I had often heard rain described as beautiful, but this was the first time I had *felt* that way about the stuff. We sought shelter with no great urgency. The river thundered by.

Ed took off his pack and sat down beside it. I studied him carefully. Was he tiring? I was still feeling fit and energetic myself, but, after all, we were six miles in—and six miles had been my limit, back in the Eagle Cap days. It was experience that had made it possible to conquer the six-mile barrier. And Ed had none. I looked around at the grove and the near meadow. This would be a good campsite, if necessary. Was it necessary?

"Three more miles," I said aloud. "You up to it?"

Ed shrugged. "If you are," he said.

"Sure? We could camp here, if—"

"Do you want to?"

"Well, it's an awfully long way from the mountain."

"Then let's not. You ready to start?"

I looked at the rain. It was still misting down, but it didn't look

very vicious. We could walk in it. I set down my pack and dug my
rain gear out of it. Ed watched but made no move toward his own.
He would walk in the rain without it. Cooling, he said. We started.

It was pleasant walking in the rain, fresh-smelling and sweet. The
clouds were high, and views were not obscured. We passed a steep
white stream plunging loudly down an unnamed mountain. The big
dark pyramid of Cusick came into view for the first time. "Goal," I
said, gesturing. Ed nodded. "Doesn't look too bad." The trail
dropped into trees, climbed out again. We ascended through a
slanting green meadow above a timbered valley. It looked oddly
familiar. Something made me turn my head to look at Craig Mountain. There it stood—a long ribbed ridge of rock with a sharp little
peak in the middle of it not unlike the head of a crouching lion.

"Ed," I screamed. "Ed—*that's it!*"

Ahead of me, Ed turned around. "That's what?" he asked,
politely.

I explained—the picture book, the gas station handout, the road
map, my long search; the scene that had for so many years meant
Wallowas; *"Right there,"* I said. Ed listened. "Oh," he said, when I
was done. And thus, before an unappreciative audience, in a gentle
rain, up a long wilderness canyon in the Wallowas, a distant and
unfinished chapter of my boyhood came at last to its long-delayed
completion. Craig Mountain! Who would have thought?

And standing in the exact spot that the pack train had occupied in
that well-memorized photo, I persuaded Ed to take my picture.

The remainder of the trip was almost anticlimactic, though I'm
sure it did not seem that way to Ed, and it will take a little while to
tell. We climbed, then contoured above cliffs. Cusick Mountain
disappeared behind lower but closer terrain. The trail passed
through a narrow spot where the river foamed and thundered, then
climbed into a spectacular little basin, flat floored, with thousand-
foot-tall, perfectly vertical walls of white limestone over which thin
pencils of waterfalls descended, blowing away into mist. The basin
was banked with snow; the trail disappeared under it. Up and
around to the right, in the next basin, would be Frazier Lake.
"Snowed in, too, most likely," I commented to Ed, looking around
at the incredible amount of snow in this lower basin. "Let's camp
here."

We found a small open grove with a crude sign labeling it Camp James. The river tossed by. Above the snowbanks and the white, waterfall-laced cliffs to the south, above what would surely be Frazier Lake, the earth gathered itself and leaped into a sharp, immediate pinnacle of purest blue-white, laced by the red vein of a basalt dike, spectacular and close. It was only a minor outrider of Cusick Mountain, but with the main peak hidden, this satellite took on a scale and a grandeur that made it seem the biggest thing in the world. It looked terribly steep. Ed gazed at it for a long time.

"If that's where we're going," he announced at last, "I'm not."

I assured him that the main peak was probably easier. We went to bed, still under clouds and with a cold wind blowing down the valley from distant snowbound rapids.

The next day was a very different day; the cliffs shone pink under a cloudless sunrise, and the song of the rapids hung distant and muted on the still air. The matches were soggy and would not light. Breakfast was cold. We ate it rapidly; we were anxious to get on our way, get moving, get warm. We crossed the wide floor of our basin and climbed beside rapids into sun. Frazier Lake stretched before us, surrounded by snow and choked with pack ice. Over it hung the huge, uncompromising shape of Glacier Peak, Eagle Cap's nearest neighbor. The sunlight danced and dazzled.

Crossing the wide outlet on a convenient logjam, we bore away from the lake, up and to the left, along a steep little ledge that slashed diagonally through the cliffs from top to bottom at an angle that probably exceeded forty-five degrees. It was exhilarating climbing on firm rock with fantastic exposure above the lake. The last thirty feet or so steepened to near verticality, but the holds were big and plentiful; nothing difficult about it. A quick scramble and I was up. Ed took longer, hugging the inside of the ledge where the holds were worse but the exposure less extreme. Watching him, I had the distinct and eerie feeling of standing beside myself. On Eagle Cap, that had been *me* on the inside. I looked over now to where Eagle Cap rose, cold and magnificent, above the walls of the Frazier Lake Basin. *You've come a long way in four years, my son,* said Eagle Cap.

Now there was a broad polished shelf of level rock, then more snow, great masses of it, sweeping up to the perfect bare pinnacle of Cusick. Its apex was still a good twelve hundred feet above us.

The snow and the sky and the dazzling rock were too bright. I reached for my goggles only to find I had left them in camp. Ed's were missing, too. In the austere and dazzling brightness of this world above timberline, this was a dangerous mistake. With my hunting knife, I carved small chunks of wood with slits in them, such as I had heard the Eskimos use. I was no Eskimo; it didn't work. Holes in our stocking caps, pulled down over our eyes? That didn't work, either. In the end we decided to stick mostly to the rock, where the glare would be least intense. We crossed snow to the base of a high, blue-white, polished cliff, an arm of the peak's northwest ridge, thrusting toward us. Five hundred feet of snow-climbing in a shadowed, cold couloir brought us to the crest of the cliff. A narrow band of smooth, glacier-worn rock, magnificent in its starkness, stretched before us. We walked along it. The peak approached. It towered over us.

Now the ridge began to grow steeper; there would be about a hundred feet of face to get up, in some way, before the easier terrain of the Northwest Ridge would confront us. I was contemplating this problem and had just about finished picking a route through it when Ed—who had remained silent since we topped the couloir—announced, quite suddenly and firmly, "Well, this is as far as I go."

I suppose I acted astonished. "Tired?" I asked.

He nodded.

"Well, let's rest here a bit, and then we can go on."

"*You* can go on."

"But you can't stop here! We're only half an hour at the most from—"

"Look," he exploded, almost angrily, "I don't want to keep you from your summit. Go on, finish your climb. I'll wait here."

I stared at him, my thoughts churning. What a ridiculous thing to happen! The summit was a mere five- or six-hundred feet above us, the hour was early, the sky was clear, the mountain beckoned—and here was my climbing companion saying he wasn't going any further. I knew the rules of the game. I had read James Ramsey Ullman. *Never split up the party, under whatever circumstances. A party is only as fast as its slowest member. The summit is less important than the welfare of the individual climber.* I knew all these, had seen them prove their worth: a storm on Sacajawea, a damaged knee on Deadman Point, lost footing on the side of Joseph—potential tragedies, all nipped in the bud because of the rules. And the first rule was: Never break the others. Still. . . .

"You sure you'll be all right?" I asked.

"I'm sure. Go on."

I took off my knapsack and dropped it on the rocks at Ed's feet. "That has the first aid kit and the lunch in it," I told him. "You may need it before I get back. Stay off the snow."

"I'm not going anywhere. Don't worry."

"It's a long ways down and it's steep, and you don't have an axe. Don't try to go down till I get back. All right?"

He nodded. "All right."

"OK, I'm on my way. Be back in about an hour. Watch the way I go in case you want to follow."

There had been too damn many failures in my recent mountain past. Rules or no rules, James Ramsey Ullman or no, I was not going to give up the summit of Cusick Mountain!

As it turned out, half an hour was an overestimate of the time required, and I was actually on top in less than twenty minutes. It was easy. The lower part of the face—call it the shoulder—was only a steep talus-scramble. The upper part was steeper and loose, but there was a way to avoid it. I moved to the right, horizontally across steep snow, to a prominent dike perhaps thirty feet away; and, left hand and foot on the dike, right foot on the snow, right hand using the ice axe, I climbed rapidly upward and onto the ridge. The ridge was a pile of shale. I ran up it.

The summit was mine.

And six-hundred feet below me, Ed—who would still be there when I returned and would get down safely but would never again try to climb a mountain—Ed set up a great whooping cry of joy, doing a little victory dance, as if he and not I had been the one to complete his first successful climb since Pete's Point. I waved back at him, more than sharing his delight.

The top of a mountain you have just climbed, after years of failures, is unequivocally the most beautiful spot in the world.

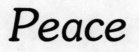

Peace

I

In late July my brother and I set out to climb Elkhorn Peak, that massive, Romanesque hump of granite that dominates the lower section of the West Lostine trail. Our departure from Pullman was delayed, and by the time we had driven to the mountains, shouldered the packs, locked the car, and set forth upon the trail, it was nearly five in the afternoon. The mountain rose before us, huge and warm in the polished and transparent light. We contoured its east flank on the river-level trail. The meadows at the mouth of Copper Creek were occupied; I had thought, halfway, of camping there, but now I proposed that we push on to a small unnamed lake sitting on Elkhorn's east shoulder a half mile above us. Jack agreed. We forded the swollen, swirling, waist-deep Lostine and climbed cross-country up a steep, sparsely timbered granite slope to the trailless shelf holding the lake. The light had turned orange. The lake was a small one, three or four acres at most, cupped in meadows, with a waterfall-laced rock garden dipping into it from the west. Conifers on the north and east edges of the meadow shelf were silhouetted in black against the void, and beyond it lay the flame-colored walls of the Lostine Canyon. Snow shelved over the lake and floated in it. We pitched our tent.

I kindled a fire; Jack half filled an aluminum pan with water, stirred powdered soup mix into it, and set it over the flames. Soon it was bobbling cheerily away. It was supposed to simmer for twelve minutes. Idly, I munched cheese and watched the southern horizon. A cloud was blossoming there. As I stared at it, it grew, burgeoned, towered upward into the sunset, detached itself from the horizon, and came racing toward us, trailing ragged black streamers. A wind gusted suddenly to life; there were several quick spatters of rain. I dove for the tent. Jack lingered, covering the soup. "'Come on!" I shouted. The rain increased, and Jack leaped in beside me. We crouched in the tent. Wind tore at it; rain pounded on it, rattling on the thin nylon shell. A crescendo of storm noises. Lightning flashed, lighting the tent in eerie blue, accompanied by a simultaneous and nearly deafening thunderclap. The strike could not have been more than a few feet away. Rain pounded furiously, then more quietly. The sound of it died away. The wind quit. Cautiously, we poked our heads out. The cloud was racing northward, still trailing its streamers. Overhead, the sky was clear, and the first stars were coming out.

Somewhat shakily, we took stock. The fire was out; though the storm had lasted barely five minutes, the ashes were already cold. The lid had blown off the soup, and the pot, which we had left half full, was overflowing into the dead fire. The soup looked rather diluted. Our sleeping bags had been in the tent with us and were dry, but everything else looked as if it had been floating in the lake.

Jack said, "Should I rekindle the fire?"

"No," I replied. I was thinking. That Lostine crossing we had made about an hour ago was kind of tricky. The current was deep and powerful, and we had each come perilously close to losing our footing and being swept into the rapids that waited a mere twenty yards or so downstream. And we had been told that this particular spot was the easiest crossing in the area. Now, suppose—just suppose—that several more storms like the one we had just been through came up, or a single larger one; enough to raise the river six or eight inches. Could we get across at all?

"I think," I said aloud, "that we'd better pack this camp up and go back down by the river. I think we may want to get back across it first thing tomorrow morning. Otherwise we may not make it."

We loaded our packs and fled down the hill in the darkness, back to the edge of the white and muttering river.

I slept very poorly that night; I kept feeling the Lostine about my legs, pushing against my waist, bowling me over. The night crept.

Eventually dawn arrived, pooling in the east and flowing down the western mountains. A perfect and a cloudless dawn. My worries had been unnecessary; we would make it back after all. And there was still plenty of time to climb the mountain, if we so desired.

We did not so desire. Our summit ardor had been quenched by the rain, quenched as thoroughly and as coldly as our fire had been. We did set out, climbing in a rather lackadaisical manner back up the lower flank of the peak, back toward the lake, which, we had now learned (from the party occupying the meadows at the mouth of Copper Creek), was called Sky; but it was climbing with no great joy. It was barely nine when we reached the lake, and the summit was just two hours above us at the most. But we had had it. We would go no further.

And now, curiously enough, a great peace came over me. Now that I had made a conscious decision to forego the summit, the summit and what it represented seemed to lose all importance and all value. What was important and valuable was not climbing but simply *being*—not being on the mountain, not being by the lake, not even being alive, but just *being*, with no modifiers and no purpose. We roamed the lake shelf in the blue morning, the sun warming through us, the earth under our feet. The lake was perfect, the surrounding mountains little less so. We drank deeply of the chilled inflow streams, lying on our chests amid flowers. The act of breathing seemed one of the fine arts.

After a while—an hour or two, or maybe a moment, or maybe a day—we left the lake and descended, without hurry, to the edge of the singing river. We loaded the packs and strapped them on. There was still the uncertainty of the crossing to be faced. For a short while we stood and looked at the trail, plunging into the deep and swirling water, climbing out again on the far bank. . . .

A short time only. Then I smiled. Though we had spent millennia by the lake, by clock time it was still early on this same July day. "Come on," I said. "We'll look for an easier crossing." And we set out upstream, through the meadows, under the mountains, watching the clear and flowing stream.

A quarter of a mile or less upstream, the river spread out and rippled quietly over a gravel bar, knee deep from bank to bank. Our boots around our necks, we waded. On the far bank, with the last remaining urgency behind us, we lay on our backs in the meadows and gazed into the domeless sky. The mountains smiled. Time flowed past us but did not touch us. A year or an age ago, when Conrad White and Bill Meyers and I had first come upon these meadows, I had dreamed of relaxing here indefinitely, without the push of a goal to urge me on. Now that dream had arrived, and unlike many dreams it was not suffering from being made flesh. My pulse slowed to the pace of the river; my back grew roots to the soil. I became the Wallowas, and the Wallowas became me. Overhead the sun swam like a separate fragment of my warm and living brain.

We breathed the scent of pines and the river.

We watched the bees working the tremulous and eager flowers.

We skipped cool stones across the fragile water.

And after a while, easily and with no sense of departure, we strapped on the packs once more and went forth along the river to the waiting car.

In August I grew a goatee.

In September I entered graduate school.

In October, word leaked up to Pullman that Cliff Olin was home from Columbia and back at Whitman for a final year. I drove down to welcome him back. We walked the streets of Walla Walla in the cool fall evening, going nowhere, Cliff striding eagerly and purposefully anyway, like a paroled prisoner. "You have no idea," he repeated over and over, "what it feels like to be able to *breathe* again." He had not enjoyed New York. "How are things back there?" I had asked once, over the phone, shortly after he arrived. His response was instantaneous. "Grimy and shitty," he said. "The buildings are grimy and shitty, the streets are grimy and shitty, the people are grimy and shitty—you name it, it's grimy and shitty." Now he was back and anxious to return to the mountains. We began planning for the coming summer.

In December, Larry Chitwood got married. I served as one of the ushers; Ron Wolff was best man. Cliff was in the congregation. We had all lost track of Bob Zimmerman.

In April my cat died.

In May I shaved off my goatee.

In June, for the first time, I paid a visit to the southern side of the

Wallowa Mountains. I have chosen the term *visit* carefully, for this was neither a climb nor a hike but something more in the nature of a lark. We were trying, I suppose—the seven of us—to prove that the world was not yet too much with us. The place: Cornucopia, a ghost town from Oregon's not-so-distant gold-mining past. The players:

John Riskin, English teacher. Ex-resident (along with Cliff Olin and Ron Wolff and myself) of a boarding establishment called The Gingerbread House in Walla Walla.

Barb Riskin, John's wife. The only one among us who had never attended Whitman.

Steve Otto, ethnomusicologist. Close friend of Larry Chitwood during our common freshman year at Whitman; collaborator with me (that same year) on a musical comedy that never got beyond the first five pages. Later, John Riskin's roommate at the University of Washington.

Curtis Smith, pianist. Spoke fluent German, a skill that he and Larry Chitwood and I had once exploited—much to the consternation of a number of nonbilingual store clerks—on a rather sprightly shopping trip through downtown Yakima, Washington.

Larry Chitwood.

Karen Chitwood.

Me.

The events of that day should probably be left largely untold—that being the kind of day it was. I will, however, give you enough to get the flavor. We arrived, all of us, in a single vehicle, a Volkswagen camper belonging to John and Barb Riskin. The hour was noonish, the weather was mixed clouds and sun. The ruins of the town stretched forth beneath tailing-splashed granite peaks. The mine buildings were locked up tight, but some of the other structures were open. Larry climbed to the second-floor balcony of the Copia Tavern and had us all take his picture, sitting on the balcony rail. Standing in the middle of Main Street, little (five-foot-four) Steve Otto lit up the biggest cigar I have ever seen, fourteen inches long and a full inch and a half in diameter. We took his picture, too. Curtis Smith found a fireplug in what used to be the residential district and, after making sure the girls were safely occupied at something else, opened his fly and did a splendid imitation of a dog.

Toward evening we walked up, away from the town, along a rough road that had once led to a mine called Queen of the West. The road lay in the valley of Pine Creek, a typical Wallowa glacial canyon, steep walled and flat floored, its head chopped off by an abrupt, towering mass of ragged maroon rock. Snowfields hung in the crags; waterfalls cascaded from them. Once this valley must have rivaled the Lostine or the Hurricane for wilderness grandeur, but it would be a long time before that rivalry could be reestablished. The valley floor lay in ruins. What had once been meadows were covered with haphazard, nondescript piles of naked and broken rock. Pieces of rusty machinery and lengths of fraying cable lay about. The creek whispered mournfully in an unnatural channel. Fully half of the gold ever mined in Oregon—many millions of dollars worth—had come out of this valley. And the valley would never be the same.

I walked apart from the others, my mood suddenly serious, looking at the wrecked meadows, looking back at the town. Had the mountains been damaged by this? In one sense, certainly, the answer had to be no. The outline of the peaks around me was unchanged; the dying sun still danced on snowfields, the snowfields still fed the waterfalls, the waterfalls still caressed their granite beds. Trees still hung in impossible places, flowers still graced the slopes. Trails led off to lakes and distant peaks. If only you kept your eyes up. . . .

But where do you draw the line? Where do you stop? Can you keep your eyes up forever? I thought of the meadows at the mouth of Copper Creek and contrasted them with what was left of these. Think of lying on your back amidst these rock piles. Think of skipping stones across this sterile and bankless creek. In the Copper-Lostine Meadows I had been part of something big and warm and complex called life. Where was the life to be part of here?

There will be those who will say that all this is irrelevant. Minerals must be taken where they are found. We like pretty places too, they will say; it is regrettable that they must be damaged. But we won't tear down the entire mountain. There is really very little change in the scenery. Just a few extra rocks in the meadow. Why are you yelling so?

You try, patiently, to explain to them. It is not really the scenery you are concerned about. It is the flowers and the grasses and the whole complex living organism that the valley once was. It is the roots that grow out of your back when you lie down by the stream. It is—

But they interrupt you. Is *that* it, they say. Why, you needn't worry about *that.* If the grass and the flowers and the streambank are so important to you, *we'll put it all back.* We will use the latest reclamation techniques to restore the overburden and plant it with pretty flowers. Just watch.

And now you know that there is no use talking further; that you exist, the two of you, on entirely separate planets and that your conversation can never meet. For when the complex and eternal animal of the soil is referred to casually as "overburden"; when it is assumed that a flower is a *flower,* not a single, nonseparable part of a great, slowly changing pattern that has been gradually working its way toward something unknowable, even to itself, since the close of the last ice age; when these things occur, then you may be using the same vocabulary, but you are talking an entirely different language. You can try to explain. You can point out, somewhat sarcastically, that the architects of reclamation can no more bring back a valley than the beauticians employed by a mortuary can bring back the people they work on. But your explanations will fall on deaf ears. Your only salvation is that these people live by the rules. And the rules can be changed.

Perhaps (looking at the tailings, looking at the sad-voiced creek, looking toward the distant and waiting mountains), *perhaps I should begin to devote some time to changing those rules.*

We climbed a pile of rock to a pile of boards that had once been a cable terminal. The cable was still intact and in place, a car hanging from it a little way up, rusted and broken and rather solemn and sad. Nearby in the rubble I spotted a piece of white quartz bearing cubical golden crystals nearly a quarter of an inch on a side. Iron pyrites—fools' gold. I picked it up and put it in my pocket. Somehow, in the context of these surroundings, the name seemed symbolic of something far more important, in the general run of the world's commerce, than a common and essentially worthless compound of iron and sulfur.

We wandered back to the car, to a big supper of beans, bacon, and beer. Then we drove home.

Two weeks later I crowned my Wallowa experience and the days of my youth by standing at last on the summit of Sacajawea.

It was a cold summit, with clouds like thick blankets hanging over it and a wind blowing. It was a nondescript sort of place, nothing much more than a heap of yellow rock rubble crowned by somebody's warped idea of what a cairn ought to be. There was no water; there was no snow; there were no flowers; there was not much of anything at all. In fact, that ragged little hump of stones had only one significant attribute, one characteristic to set it aside and make people wish to seek it out: It was higher than anything else for several hundred miles in any direction. And even that distinction was almost fudged. A mile to the south, massive and square against the storm, the Matterhorn came to within seven feet of beating it.

I stood by the summit cairn, my hands in my pockets and my shoulders hunched against the cold and gusting wind, looking down at the distant world. It was an inhospitable-appearing place. Snow lay heavily over most of what I could see; clouds hung heavily above that. A few yards west of my feet the mountain dropped off suddenly, leaping downward into cliffs, the cliffs plunging into the great tilted snowfields that form the floor of the Northwest Cirque. Beyond the cirque was the deep, airy canyon of the Hurricane. And in that canyon, four thousand feet beneath us, almost invisibly tiny, was a small gray speck. I couldn't see any detail on it at that distance, of course, but I didn't need to. I had put it there myself. It was my tent.

From someplace close behind me came a soft clicking *whirrrrr . . .* like the sound of a giant metallic insect. It was Cliff Olin's movie camera; he was filming our ascent route, most of which was visible from where we stood. From the tent, pitched on a shelf by a waterfall several hundred feet up the west wall of the canyon, we had dropped down, crossed Hurricane Creek on fallen logs, and ascended the mountain's timbered west flank. The outlet stream from the cirque cascaded beside us. We entered the cirque itself at about 7,600 feet; by chance rather than design, the point of entry led us directly through the site of our retreat camp in 1963, the camp we had set up following our tussle with the blizzard, our almost-victory over the mountain, and the lost sleeping bag incident. There was nothing left there to see, only the ghosts of memories. We climbed on. An hour later, high in the cirque, on an endless pile of moraine beside an endless snowfield, we stopped for lunch. As we ate, the sky swooped down on us, flipping the calendar back. Snow fell. We finished lunch in a small blizzard, unable to see more than twenty or thirty feet in any direction. Then the storm departed, as rapidly as it had come. Above the moraines, tucked back under the summit cliffs, was a great curving bowl of snow—all that was left of the glacier that had made the moraines and the cliffs. We crossed the bowl and climbed the far side. Here we had a short argument. I wanted, for symbolic reasons, to climb snowfields up and to the left, joining our old summit route at the point we had left it and completing the climb along our original route. Cliff wanted, for aesthetic reasons, to climb directly up the face. The gray wind blew; clouds scudded close above us, disappearing behind the towering summit. We settled the argument rapidly, though the solution was one I'm sure the American Alpine Club wouldn't approve of: We split up, each going his own way. Forty-five minutes later we met on the summit. The climb was over.

Now what?

I waited for the usual summit elation. It did not come. *Why not?* This trip was supposed to be the climax, the consummation of my Wallowa days. The top. The highest spot in the Wallowas: for that matter, the highest nonvolcanic spot in the Pacific Northwest. The only things higher were the big volcanic cones over in the Cascades. I was literally on top of my world. Two attempts, two failures. And then, on the third try, success. Why didn't I feel successful? Goddammit, I was being cheated! What was wrong?

Well, maybe I could pin down a reason or two. Or at least speculate. There was, to begin with, the matter of other people. On every mountain I had ever climbed, my party had been the only one present. Even when you knew others had been there—in the case of a peak like Hood or Eagle Cap, many others—there was still a feeling of isolation, of attaining a goal sought by many but achieved by few. There was conquest, through skill and endurance, of something unconquerable by the general run of humanity. But this feeling was impossible to obtain on this Fourth of July on Sacajawea.

We were far from alone. A party of four was leaving just as we arrived; a party of two arrived shortly after us. A third party was on its way. These others had all come up the easy way, from Ice Lake; we alone had come up from the Hurricane. That was something, but it was not enough. The damn summit felt about as private and as unconquerable as Grand Central Station.

So people were a part of the problem. But they weren't the whole problem: Gazing down the Northwest Ridge, I could see that there was something else still bothering me.

The climb had been too easy.

I remembered 1963, remembered it all too clearly: the snow, and the wind that blew it at us high on a ridge above the world; a toothache, and the cry of a panther in a night-encircled canyon; our two-camp assault on the great mountain; a timberline camp on the blue edge of morning, and the black enigma of the buttress, and the perilous, icy course around it. I remembered the thrill of achievement that had coursed through us when at last we attained the North Summit and saw, through the blurred and blowing sky, the true summit stark and close and within our grasp. And most of all, I remembered the way that thrill had been punctured and shown to be hollow. One split second—that was all it had taken. One split second and one poorly anchored pack strap. A sleeping bag, whirling away to nothing down a black-and-white, windy slope. A last desperate attempt to reach the summit. A huge black step. And failure.

But what a magnificent failure!

And as for today's success? Nothing. A walk-up. Three miles of steep uphill hiking, five hundred feet of snow climbing, which my increasingly confident ice-axe technique rendered little more difficult or perilous than a trail. Or a sidewalk, for that matter. It was a success, yes; the summit had been reached. But it was an empty, fizzled sort of success. The giant firecracker had gone off, but it had turned out to be a cardboard mock-up with only a ladyfinger inside.

Cliff came to stand beside me, and together, from our mediocre summit, we looked down on our glorious almost-summit. The high point we had reached was barely fifty easy-looking yards away. We couldn't see the step, of course—it faced the other way—but we could see plenty of routes around it. Easy routes—walk-ups. The hour we had figured on from below suddenly shrunk to less than ten minutes. We could have made it! Had we only known. . . .

Cliff said, with marvelous simplicity and eloquence, Shee-*it*.

"Next time," I told him, "remember to tighten your pack strap *first.*"

We turned away from the past and started down.

The descent was a different world.

The climb had been future oriented, looking toward the summit and expecting too much of it. The summit itself had been past oriented, looking backward down a long cold ridge through a phantom blizzard to a ghostly, tumbling sleeping bag. But the descent was free of both the past and the future. The descent had only itself and the now of each second to look to. And on the descent I recaptured the Wallowas.

There was a glissade—at least a thousand feet of glissade—steep and joyous and bounding, my ice axe acting as a part of me, adding the pleasure of a tool well used to the pure flying ecstasy of the slide itself.

There was a walk across acres of almost level névé in the vast cold shadow of the mountain, a walk in an arctic of tall rock and treeless, ancient snow—a walk climaxed by the discovery, far on the south side of the great cirque, of a small glacial pond of ice-blue water, snow for its floor, its far end lapping the tumbled, raw detritus of what must surely be the youngest moraine on the mountain.

There was a drink of pure, cold snowmelt issuing from the blue depths of a cave in the snout of the protoglacier; a drink, once more, of something more than water: of earth juice, of nectar, of the essence and the soul of Sacajawea.

And finally, far down the cirque, almost out of it, there was a moment that approached magic. We were sitting on the lowest and oldest of the moraines, taking a breather and a last look around before plunging into the closed-in forest. I was looking, I believe, mostly at rocks. The discovery of those iron pyrites crystals at Cornucopia had whetted my latent rock-hound instincts, and here, on this huge pile of unsorted hand-size specimens at the bottom of the cirque, those instincts were receiving full play. Cliff watched me idly. Suddenly, he said, "Goats."

"What?" I asked, not quite comprehending.

"Mountain goats," said Cliff. He was looking at something over my left shoulder. Slowly, I turned to look too.

About twenty feet below the crest of the south wall, less than a hundred yards away from us, three large, shaggy, exceedingly solemn-eyed creatures looked back.

Cliff was reaching, very slowly, for his binoculars. "They just came over from the south," he said. "I don't think they expected to see anyone here. They stopped very suddenly when they saw us. Don't make any rapid movements."

"I wasn't planning to," I breathed. "Listen, Cliff, I'm going to try to get close enough for a picture. They're going to see me coming, and they're going to run. But don't do anything that will scare them off early. Maybe if only *one* of us moves toward them. . . ."

"Go ahead, I'll watch 'em from here." Cliff had the glasses to his eyes and was adjusting the eyepieces. *"Jeesh"* (like a soft explosion), "what a big old billy. . . ."

I moved my camera around in front of my breastbone, opened the case, and popped up the waist-level viewer. No telephoto—that meant I was going to have to get awfully damn close. I set shutter speed and f-stop. And then, my hands on the camera, one finger poised over the shutter release, my eyes fixed on the goats, I began walking slowly across the moraine directly toward them.

Two of the goats hastened quickly back over the rim, disappeared, then cautiously poked their heads back into view to watch my approach. The third—the lead billy that Cliff had exclaimed over—held his ground and watched me coming. The distance closed to eighty yards, then sixty. Still no move. Fifty yards. And, at last, motion.

Slowly, the big billy pivoted about on his tiny ledge. For a fraction of a moment our eyes met and held. A heartbeat. Then I dropped my sight to the viewfinder, and the goat went scrambling. Rock fragments rattled under his feet. My shutter clicked. He was up and over. The mountain was empty.

I walked slowly back to where Cliff was waiting. "You scared him away," he said as I approached. I said nothing, because there wasn't anything to say. There was no way that I could possibly explain to Cliff that he was wrong, and that I *knew* he was wrong. I had met the old billy's eyes. Eyes can be extremely powerful organs of communication, even between individuals of different species, as anyone who has ever lived intimately with a dog or a cat will be able to confirm. And these eyes had held no fear. No anxiety. A trace of mild annoyance, perhaps. But mostly—and I say this with full knowledge that I will be accused of being entirely too anthropomorphic, of reading too much of my own reaction into that of a lower animal—mostly there was dignity. Dignity, and a simple desire to be alone.

That goat had not fled because he was afraid. That goat had left because he didn't like me. Because he wanted to be by himself.

I know, I know. No proof—no proof, and no way to prove it. Very well. Let me drop half the statement. *The goat was not afraid.* That I know. Fear is one of the easiest emotions to read. There was no fear here. Call it simply a reaction. He was going elsewhere and did not wish to linger.

As were we. As did we.

Kin to a goat. The goat as kin, as friend, as brother.

It would be perfect, for the sake of the narrative, to be able to say that it was at this very moment that I realized at last the answers to the questions that I had asked long ago on Pete's Point. It would be perfect to be able to say that I had found the wholeness I had only vaguely sensed then; that I had found why wilderness was so important; that I had seen, with blinding clarity, how I fitted into the world and how the world fitted into me. But of course I didn't. Realization is not a sudden thing, and it would be some time before I could begin to fit the events of this day into the fabric and design of my understanding. Just then, I knew only this: that the questions were still important. Not for their answers—I didn't even know if they had any answers—but for themselves. Because it is questions such as these that make us human. Because the world will have lost more than it can afford to lose when we have forgotten how to ask them.

I put on my knapsack.

I stood awhile, looking at the spot where the goat had vanished.

And after a while I turned and followed Cliff, into the forest, beside the stream, down from the disappointment and overanticipation of the summit into the calm deliverance of the world.

Epilogue

Why do we need wilderness?

There are any number of answers to that question, any number of good practical reasons that may be cited to prove the desirability of preserving large tracts of land in a natural state. We can speak, for example, of the very real and urgent need of science for wilderness, both as a point of reference and as a subject for study in its own right. Nature has been in business for more than four billion years; it is inconceivable that something that has been under development for that extraordinary length of time can have revealed all its secrets to the human mind in the mere two hundred and fifty years or so since the dawning of modern science. And even if it had, there would remain a need for what the biologist Luna Leopold refers to as "bench marks," undisturbed areas against which to measure the disturbances caused by humanity. The need for control groups has long been recognized in the social sciences and in the medical sciences; it is every bit as necessary in the land sciences. As Leopold once remarked, "To describe a biota there is no substitute for a sample." Therefore it is essential to preserve as many types of samples as possible. And since we cannot be certain that any one of these samples will remain unchanged when taken out of its natural context, it is important to preserve the context as well.

We can speak of the need to preserve as many different species of plants and animals as possible, for the simple and utterly selfish reason that one never knows which of them are going to prove valuable to us. The classic example of this is, of course, bread mold, which gave us penicillin. Suppose bread mold—which would certainly qualify as a household pest—should have been eliminated before Alexander Fleming was born? Or to choose another example: Suppose the ladybird beetle, which preys on aphids and other insect pests, should be exterminated. Would not the economic harm alone be incalculable? Would not humanity's loss be irredeemable if it had killed off the dog instead of domesticating it because it competed with humans for game? Without the example of the birds, would we ever have learned to fly?

Or again, we can speak of the need for wilderness as diversity. Any economist can tell you that the healthiest economy is one that is diversified as much as possible. It takes little imagination to see that the same is of necessity true of ecological systems. The Tussock moth, for instance, which eats only Douglas fir needles, is a much greater threat to pure stands of Douglas fir than it is to mixed stands of Douglas fir, true fir, hemlock, spruce, larch, and pine.

Yet another area where wilderness has great practical value is in the field of watershed management. It is axiomatic that an undisturbed watershed will produce a steadier flow of cleaner water than will one in which humanity's influence has been felt. This is why the watershed of Ashland Creek—from which the community I live in, here in Oregon, gets its drinking water—has been declared off limits to logging, to road building, even to overnight camping. It is why the state of New York set aside the Adirondack Forest Preserve, the largest state park in America. It is why the city of Walla Walla, even back when I was at Whitman, would not even allow *day* use of the watershed of Mill Creek. Not long ago I drove with three Forest Service employees along an unimproved road in the Siskiyou Mountains during a major rainstorm. We crossed several creeks, large and small, coming down to the road from the undisturbed slopes of Wagner Butte; these were all running clear. Then we came to a stream, Wagner Creek, which paralleled the road for a long distance. It was running thick and brown with mud. The value of wilderness to water quality could not have been more clearly or graphically presented.

All of these—science, potential practical value, diversity, watershed protection—are important reasons for the preservation of wilderness. Any one, in fact, would be sufficient cause to preserve as much wild land as is practical. But there is another need, another value that may be more important than all of these. It is the value that is the real driving force behind wilderness preservation, the value for which the other needs have been brought forth as rationalizations. And it is the value that drives us to preserve as much wild land as is *possible*—not practical.

This value is the need for wilderness as a resource of the spirit. We need wilderness not only for what it can do for us but for what it can mean to us. We need the wilderness to grow up in.

We need the challenge of wilderness. We need places where only the few can go, not only for those few but for the rest of us as well. We need the continuance of possibility; we need the certain knowledge that at least part of the Earth is not broken to harness but remains stern and adventurous and demanding. That map is cramping and soul constricting that has no places that may be labeled: *Here there bee tygers.* For such places keep alive the possibility that each person who enters them may be the discoverer of something that no one else in the world has ever found, and it is this potential for discovery that is our principal excuse, after all, for being human. Wild places, therefore, are our most important keys to the large promise of the future; they are, as Wallace Stegner so aptly put it in his book *Beyond the Hundredth Meridian,* "a part of the geography of hope."

We need the humility that the wilderness teaches, the sensation that Herbert Weiner once described as "infinite littleness before overwhelming Power." We need to know how small we are. We need to be reminded, every so often, that we are not the only creatures on this planet but merely one among many; that we have inherited from its Maker a world of magnificent scope and complexity and beauty; and that the world that people have built around themselves, the world of cities and fields and roads and geometrically perfect landscapes, is only an artifice of—to quote Terry and Renny Russell's book *On the Loose*—"comfortable and incorrect proportions." The story is told of Theodore Roosevelt that, during the last years of his life, at his Sagamore Hill estate on Long Island, he would go outdoors each clear evening about bedtime, taking whoever might be in the house with him, and all would scan the stars until they had located that tiny fuzzy patch in the constellation Andromeda that is known as the Great Andromeda Galaxy. Facts would be reeled off: "The galaxy is 4 quintillion miles away; it is 600 quadrillion miles across and 50 quadrillion miles thick; it contains 40 billion stars; its light, traveling so fast that it could circle the Earth seven and one-half times each *second*, takes 680 thousand *years* to reach us." There would be a few moments of silence. Then Roosevelt would say: "I guess we feel small enough for tonight. Let's go to bed." It is certainly no coincidence that the man who could devise this exercise was among this country's first—and greatest—conservationists.

But even more than the challenge of wilderness, and the humility it teaches, we need the integration and the wholeness that only an experience of wildlands can provide. This is something that is virtually impossible to describe to one who has not experienced it for himself. In *My First Summer in the Sierra* John Muir called it a sensation of being "homogeneous throughout, sound as a crystal." Your five senses seem to melt into one Sense, alert and marvelously acute; your body seems to exist not for itself but only as an extension of the great warm Body of the Earth. There is a feeling of *isness*, of rightness and completion; at the same time, there is an anticipation, an expectation, a pause on the brink of the infinite that offers glimpses of a perfect peace. Is this mysticism? Perhaps. To feel God best, get closest to what He has made. It is no accident that Eden was a garden, or that Christ spent his last night of freedom in Gethsemane. But one does not have to adhere to the postulates and the language of religion to explain this particular and striking function of wilderness. For whatever cause is postulated, an omniscient mind or the slow but inexorable workings of blind chance, the same conclusion must ultimately be reached: That the universe has design, and that this design is almost infinitely complex. Each of us is a part of that design, one cog in a vast and smoothly functioning machine. And it is in the wilderness that we feel this most surely. For we were made for the wilderness, not the city. We did not evolve in the city. Our visual acuity is most sensitive in the wavelengths corresponding to the greens and blues, our aural acuity most discriminating in a sound range extending roughly from the boom of a waterfall to the song of a bird. Our skins are marvelously complex organs, with heat receptors especially designed to draw energy from the long waves of the sun, and pressure sensors delicate enough to feel the small movements of the immaterial air, and thousands of tiny air-conditioners—the sweat glands—whose operation depends on the fact that in nature the air is seldom still. We were designed to function in the wilderness, and it is in the wilderness that we still function best. And this is the reason behind the other reasons, the strongest and most real need for all the wilderness that can possibly be preserved.

We need the wilderness because we need places where we may go to be reminded, every once in a while, of what it means to be entirely alive.

I came to the wilderness to conquer it; to prove, by the application of boot to mountainside, that there was no place on the Earth's surface where my own two legs could not take me.

I returned to the wilderness to learn from it; to discover what it was that I felt in the high and undiluted world, and what made it so important, and why it was damaged by a reservoir on the Wallowa River or a store at Aneroid Lake.

I go now to the wilderness to be a part of it; to accept my place in the world and its place in me; to grow into reality as a tree grows into the rain, to conform to the Earth as a stream conforms to the stones of its bed. To live. To aspire. To be.

Evening in camp. My companion has been fishing, drawing the round red eggs of a dead salmon through the limpid water of this eight-thousand-foot-high Maxwell Lake; he has had several strikes and has worked one ten-incher to within six feet of his waiting net before losing it, but he has landed nothing. I, who do not fish, have been wandering the shore of the lake, climbing the moraine that made it, drinking from the springs at its upper end, and admiring the high, smooth, and gently curving cliff of granite that drops into it on the south side, warmed and polished by the stark late-afternoon light. We are nearly three thousand feet above the canyon of the Lostine, riding an impossibly tiny shelf filled mostly by the lake and dominated, at its southwest corner, by a large, raw, snow-collared pinnacle of a mountain that has no name on the map and that we have chosen—because the human mind cannot function without categorizing the objects around it—to call Maxwell Point. Eastward, beyond the gulf of the canyon, the big granite rib of the Hurricane Divide cleaves the fading sky; a gap in it offers a glimpse of the white marble face of the Matterhorn, distant and pure and seeming to glow with its own cold inner light. This is my first trip to the Wallowas in more than three years, my first trip since Sacajawea, my first venture into the deep wilderness since my completion of graduate school, my marriage, the birth of my daughter, and the beginning of bondage to the large irrelevancies of the world. I am feeling rather self-conscious about the whole thing. But the Wallowas will forgive self-consciousness. They have forgiven much worse.

A fire has been built, food has been cooked and eaten, and now the fire is dying. We huddle close to it in the cooling August evening, talking of many things—of the steep trail up from the Lostine, of the way we will go tomorrow (up *that* talus slope, through *that* notch, and, we hope, on to the summit of Elkhorn Peak, two miles to the south of us), and of the vast difference between the conglomeration of bodies down at the trailhead and the total solitude we are enjoying here on the mountain. Of all things I have noticed in the wilderness, this is perhaps the hardest to understand: Why do people insist on remaining so close to their cars, as if they were tied to them by some unseverable umbilicus? The trail to Maxwell Lake begins at a Forest Service campground called Shady on the Lostine Canyon road. That campground, we had discovered upon our arrival, was full of screaming children riding bicycles, full of barking dogs, full of dust, and full of cars. There had been almost no room for us to park. And yet the trail, even at its beginning, had been utterly deserted. Squirrels had scolded from the branches; birds, hidden in the trailside bushes, had spun about us magnificent and captivating webs of song; a bear, startled at our approach, had crashed off across the hillside like a trackless express train. But there had been no people. Halfway to the lake we had met one party of three, coming down. That had been all. And now, here at the lake, beside the fire, the night is silent.

And then, suddenly, the silence is no longer so complete. There is the sound of a large and rapidly moving animal, the crackling and crashing of a heavy body through brush, the clatter of approaching hooves. As we look up, startled, a pair of deer come pounding out of the small grove to the north, a doe followed closely by a nearly full-grown fawn. They pass directly through our camp, perhaps twenty feet away from us. They do not appear to notice us.

Is some predator chasing them? Somewhat anxiously, we scan the grove from which they came. But no shape moves steathily through the twilight, no tail twitches, no eyes glow. Then what?— But we have no time to form the question further. For as suddenly as they arrived the first time, the deer return, circling back into our camp over the north shoulder of the moraine. Perhaps fifty feet from us the doe stops, so precipitously that the fawn runs into her. She strikes out at it with her rear hooves, wheels, and thunders rapidly off in a new direction. The fawn stands confused for a moment, then gallops after her. And the meaning of what we are seeing dawns, suddenly and simultaneously, upon us. The doe is trying to lose her fawn; she is sending it out into the wide world to fend for itself. She has chosen this end of Maxwell Lake as the farewell point. And so intent is she upon what she is doing that the presence of two men is irrelevant, perhaps even unnoticed.

For nearly twenty minutes we watch, fascinated, as the small drama unfolds before us. Back and forth dash the two deer, over and around the moraine, through and beside our camp, occasionally passing so close that they come between us and our tent. The doe is trying every trick in the book. She wheels on the fawn, biting at it, nudging it away, chasing it a few paces and then running off in the opposite direction. The fawn turns and follows her. She kicks out at it with her hind feet, with her forefeet. She runs in odd, feinting patterns that the fawn has difficulty following; she vanishes over the moraine, executes a sharp turn out of sight, and appears behind the fawn—quietly—while it is still rushing over the top in pursuit of her. Nothing works. Eventually the two disappear, pell-melling back into the woods from which they came, the doe still leading, the fawn still doggedly at her heels. Silence descends.

Tomorrow we will approach Elkhorn Peak. We will ascend *that* talus slope, pass through *that* notch, contour the basin beyond, and climb over snow and steep, loose rock to its far rim, emerging on the ridge directly above tiny, seldom-visited Catched Two Lake.

From nine-thirty in the morning to three-thirty in the afternoon we will remain on that ridge, battling its loose places, its ups and downs, its impenetrable patches of krummholz, coming closer and closer to the summit block of Elkhorn but never quite reaching it. But this failure will seem unimportant. For we already have memories of something much rarer than a summit to take home with us.

I poke the fire with a stick, sending sparks flying upward, riding invisible heat waves into the thin dark air. Like the fawn, I have been sent out into the world to fend for myself. And as it has been for the fawn, the wilderness has been part of the process. Unlike the fawn, however, I can—if I so choose—be cognizant of what is going on. For man is the animal that knows. And this is what makes him different.

All of us—Man, deer, tree, stone, lake, and upward-flying sparks—all of us have our roles to play. Each of us is a part of the world. Each part is significant. But only Man has the ability to comprehend that significance. We are the land's awareness of itself: That is our function, the reason for which we exist. Unless we are aware, we fail in our purpose. But, conversely, if we become aware, then no other purposes—no summits or conquests or manipulations or any of the large and unimportant goals of our lives—can mishandle us.

I have come to the wilderness to be a part of it. I have stayed because the wilderness has become a part of me.

I have come to the wilderness to learn from it and have stayed because the lesson will never be complete.

I have come to the wilderness to test my manhood. I have stayed because I have discovered my humanhood.

The fire dies. I stand up and stretch. I crawl into my sleeping bag. My thoughts turn fleetingly to my infant daughter, waiting at home with her mother, Melody—Melody of the Outing Club, of Aneroid Lake, and of the long slow trek back from Seven-Mile Camp on Eagle Creek. Melody and I have both come of age in the wilderness. Someday our daughter, too, will need the insights of wilderness, that she may also come of age. Will the places remain, that she may seek such insights? Will there be the challenge of summits, the long cool body of the lake, the dance of deer in a dark forest?

Man is the land's awareness of itself.
Man is the animal that knows—
What it means to be fully alive.

In the midst of my large home, knowing, aware, and alive, I settle quietly and serenely into sleep.

Glossary

Words set in SMALL CAPS are defined elsewhere in the glossary.

CHIMNEY. In mountaineering, a vertical rock cleft large enough to admit a person but small enough so that the person can reach from wall to wall. It is climbed with one hand and one foot on each wall; or, if the surfaces of the walls are smooth, by placing the back against one wall and the feet against the other and hitching upward, a process known as *chimneying*.

CIRQUE. A basin that holds or has recently held the head of a glacier. It has deep sides and a flat floor, rather like half a teacup. May contain lakes and/or meadows.

CLEAVER. A long, narrow rib of rock or SCREE separating two glaciers or snowfields—or two sections of the same GLACIER or snowfield. It lies in the center of a face, not at the angle where two faces meet; hence, not a true ridge.

COL. A high pass or notch in a mountain ridge. Usually confined to small gaps above timberline.

CONTOUR. (1) A line on a topographic map connecting points of equal elevation. (2) The act of walking at a steady elevation along a mountainside.

COULOIR. A steep gully on the face of a mountain. Broader than it is deep, usually floored with SCREE.

CRAMPONS. Metal frames with inch-long spikes on them, which are strapped to a climber's boots to enable him to gain traction on ice or hard snow. They are classified by the number of spikes, or *points*, that they carry: *eight-point crampons, ten-point crampons*, etc.

EXPOSURE. The distance a climber would fall should he happen to lose his grip. Used also for the distance a climber *feels* as though he would fall.

FELSENMEER. Literally, "boulder-sea." A gentle rock slope that has been cracked into large boulders by FROST-WEDGING. A felsenmeer looks much like a TALUS slope, but there is no cliff above it, and little or no motion of the talus has taken place, the cracking being accomplished in position.

FROST-WEDGING. A geological process in which water that has trickled into cracks during the day freezes at night; the expansion of the freezing water forces the cracks to become larger. Quite large pieces of rock may be split entirely away from a mountainside in this manner.

GENDARME. A pinnacle or rock sticking out of the crest of a ridge, which may occur in groups. The word means *guard* or *policeman* in French.

GLACIER. An accumulation of ice of sufficient size so that its weight makes it creep downhill; this motion is actually a flowing movement, like that of water, though of course much slower (a few inches to several feet a year).

GLISSADE. A means of descending mountains by sliding down snowfields. There are two basic forms: the *standing glissade* (in which the feet serve as skis) and the *sitting glissade* (in which the broadest portion of the human anatomy serves as a sled). Often great speeds may be reached. The ICE AXE is used as a brake and as a rudder.

ICE AXE. The snow-climber's principal tool. About three feet long, with a spike at one end of its handle and an adze-and-pick combination at the other, the axe serves as cane, brake, rudder, step-cutter, safety harness, shovel, and belay point. (Did I leave any out?)

INSTEP CRAMPONS. Small (four-point) crampons that are strapped to the boot just forward of the heel (useful only on an emergency basis).

KRUMMHOLZ. A growth form taken by trees at timberline, which keeps them small and twisted, never getting larger than a bush, though they may reach a considerable age. The term is usually applied only when a fairly large group of these trees exists, like a brush field. (An isolated tree of this type is often referred to as a *bonsai*, after the formal gardening art of Japan involving stunted trees.)

MASSIF. A bulky peak forming a distinct mass, separable from its neighbors, though it may have several distinct (and separately named) summits.

MORAINE. A deposit of unsorted rock, soil, sand, etc., dumped at the end of its journey by a receding glacier.

NÉVÉ. Highly compacted hard snow, in the process of changing to ice. The basic material of permanent snowfields and of the heads of glaciers.

RUNOUT. A level spot at the base of a snow- or SCREE-slope that is big enough to stop an out-of-control climber who slides onto it, thus preventing him from going over a cliff or into a creek or . . . ?

SCREE. Fine material (dirt, sand, gravel) forming a steep slope on a mountainside; differentiated from TALUS primarily by the size of the particles involved.

SUN CUPS. A condition of snow in which the surface has developed a pattern of deep, regular, cup-shaped pits separated by a gridwork of ridges. It is caused by . . . Well, no one knows exactly, but it seems to have something to do with *sublimation* (the process by which snow is converted directly into water vapor without passing through the liquid state at all). It occurs only late in the season at very high altitudes.

TALUS. Large rocks that have fallen from a cliff and are piled at the bottom in a steep, jumbled slope.

TRAVERSE. A route that moves across a slope instead of straight up it. Similar to a CONTOUR, except that the traverse gains or loses some elevation, while the contour remains level.

WATERBAR. A small log placed across a trail at a slant to deflect water and thus prevent erosion.